Praise for *The Pressure Code*

"Performance isn't built on motivation; it's built on systems. This book strips away the noise and delivers a clear, practical framework for performing under pressure. Grounded in real-world experience with elite performers, it will resonate across sport, business, and life. A game changer for anyone operating under pressure."

—James Laughlin, #1 International Bestselling Author,
Habits of High Performers

"Jason Stacy takes lessons he's learned from working with the best performers in the world and gives you a road map to apply them in your own life. Whether you're a beginner or deep on the path of mastery, this book will help you unlock your potential, build sustainable systems for performance, and elevate your game."

—Brad Stulberg, *New York Times* Bestselling Author,
The Way of Excellence and *The Practice of Groundedness*

"Jason has captured the absolute essence of what it takes to perform at the highest level. *The Pressure Code* isn't just another book on mindset; it's a master class in turning chaos into clarity. As a coach and lifelong martial artist, I can tell you this is the real deal, a blueprint for anyone ready to stop just fighting through life and start mastering it."

—Bobby Rich, Trusted Performance Coach to World-Class Teams
and Athletes; Judo and BJJ Black Belt; former Team
Great Britain Olympic Alternate, Judo; and Cofounder, ONUS

"Jason Stacy has distilled his hard-earned life experience and his success coaching elite athletes into a remarkable, practical framework. Forget silver bullet solutions: *The Pressure Code* is a thoughtful guide to building an internal operating system that can hold up under the greatest pressure. He shows how we can harness our energy, regulate our emotions, and influence our environment to get fully aligned. His whole career has been in the trenches of what it takes to be number one in the world, and you get the gift of learning from it."

—Anton Rabie, Cofounder and Cochairman, Spin Master,
the Global Entertainment Empire behind PAW Patrol
and other billion-dollar brands like Rubik's Cube

"An example of humility, wisdom, respect, and love for life. Jason converts the toughest life experiences into pure gold and shares them with the world, not from the point of a victim but from the point of an observer, a great student, and a great warrior."

—Marat Safin, former World #1 Men's Tennis Pro,
US Open and Australian Open Champion

"*The Pressure Code* is a system forged through real adversity and refined across decades of working with champions. Jason gets to the root of why some people perform and others plateau—and gives you a real path forward. His story alone is worth the read, but what he's built from it—a practical, proven framework helping elite performers align their energy, emotions, and environment—is genuinely transformative."

—Samantha Kwok, VP Brand and Operations, IM8

"The concept of apps versus operating systems in this book really hits home. The lessons aren't just relevant in elite sport; they translate directly into everyday life and professional environments. Improving your operating system will always outperform chasing quick fixes."

—Dan Tollenaere, Chief Executive Officer,
Derrimut 24/7 Gyms, and BJJ Black Belt

"At Platinum Mile Ventures, we operate in the highest-pressure environments—backing ideas before they're proven and making decisions when certainty doesn't exist. *The Pressure Code* reflects the reality of that world: Pressure isn't a barrier, it's the arena where conviction, discipline, and vision are tested and refined."

—Brandon Shainfeld, Founder, Platinum Mile Ventures

"In professional tennis, where coaches are replaced after a bad week, Aryna Sabalenka has had Jason Stacy by her side for seven years and counting. This book proves exactly why.

"Built from the hardest experiences possible, Jason's framework is the most precise explanation I've found for why some people hold under pressure and others don't.

"This book is the manual for anyone who has something real to lose."

—Danny Yeung CEO, Prenetics (NASDAQ: PRE) & IM8

"I've read so many books in this space, but nothing compares to this. Jason's messaging is so clear and precise—it's incredibly easy to follow. With practical strategies for balancing your energy, emotions, and environment, this book creates a foundation for purpose and consistency. A must-read for anyone seeking transformation!"

—Candice Warner, 3x World Champion (Surf Lifesaving);
Ironwoman Competitor at 14, Champion by 16; Author and
Keynote Speaker on Mindset, Resilience, and Transformation

"This isn't just for athletes and coaches. It's for CEOs, doctors, parents—anyone who wants a real framework for how they operate. Seventeen years in coaching, and Jason Stacy is still teaching me something. Sky's the limit for this book."

—Mike G, NBA Performance Coach and
Strength and Conditioning Specialist

"Whether you're competing at the highest level or making decisions that reach millions, *The Pressure Code* delivers a clear framework for staying sharp, aligned, and effective when it matters most."

—Steve Blatter, Head of Music Programming, SiriusXM/Pandora

"What's impressive about Jason is that he doesn't rely on clichés or surface-level motivation. He has built a clear, structured system for understanding how people actually perform under pressure. His concept of aligning energy, emotions, and environment resonates deeply with how high performers operate, whether in sports or business.

"*The Pressure Code* is not another book about trying harder or pushing through. It's about building the right internal system so that when pressure shows up, you respond with clarity, control, and consistency. Business leaders, executives, and entrepreneurs will recognize themselves in these pages. Like I did myself."

—Georgios Frangulis, Founder and CEO, OAKBERRY

"I first met Jason over dinner with a few other top tour coaches. As they reminisced about the start of their careers, Jason shared parts of his story that continue to shape him and his work. You could feel the shift as everyone listened. You could tell he often reassesses his life and learnings to understand others, and then naturally helps them. He is meticulous about his days while keeping it real and truly showing up for himself and the ones in his environment. It's a privilege to be part of it and to now see his mind captured in his book."

—Flavia Dechandt Araujo, Founding Partner, Unbox Sports

"So proud to see Jason crushing it on the world stage with Sabalenka! Jason has always been one of the most knowledgeable and passionate people I've ever worked with. He doesn't just coach; he changes mindsets. His book finally puts his genius on paper, and I'm certain it's going to help so many people level up their lives and careers."

—Conchita Martinez, International Tennis Hall of Famer,
Wimbledon Champion, and 2021 WTA Coach of the Year

"Jason understands that an athlete's psychology, physicality, and environment are inextricably linked, and only when these elements are balanced is true performance possible. He is always looking for the edge and constantly looking at where to improve his knowledge. He has many valuable insights which will help all athletic practitioners, no matter whether you are training Grand Slam–winning tennis players, youth sports, or anything in between. Jason is an innovator in his field."

—Jez Green, Performance Coach to Multiple Grand Slam Champions

THE PRESSURE CODE

How Elite Performers Align Their Energy, Emotions, and Environment

JASON STACY

MATT HOLT

Matt Holt Books
An Imprint of BenBella Books, Inc.
Dallas, TX

MATT HOLT BENBELLA

Matt Holt is an imprint of BenBella Books, Inc.
BenBella Books, Inc.
8080 N. Central Expressway
Suite 1700
Dallas, TX 75206
benbellabooks.com
Send feedback to feedback@benbellabooks.com

Matt Holt and *BenBella* are federally registered trademarks.

Printed in the United States of America
10 9 8 7 6 5 4 3 2 1

Library of Congress Control Number: 2026011543
ISBN 9781637749401 (hardcover)
ISBN 9781637749418 (electronic)

Editing by Sarah Modlin
Copyediting by Shelby Harbour
Proofreading by Martha Gallant and Marissa Wold Uhrina
Text design and composition by Jordan Koluch
Cover design by Jason Arias
Cover image © Adobe Stock / Mykola Mazuryk
Printed by Lake Book Manufacturing

For Kellee, Aidan, Kai, and Jada.

You are the reason I do any of this.

Every hard decision. Every moment it would've been easier to quit.
I think of you—and I find a way forward.

This work is my promise to live with purpose, to act with strong values, and to do the right thing even when no one's watching.

I hope you're proud of me.
More than that, I hope you're proud to be part of this family.

Contents

Foreword by Aryna Sabalenka xi

Introduction 1

1. From Fighter to Warrior 9
2. The Sweet Spot of Performance 23
3. Energy: The Currency of Performance 33
4. Emotions: Signals, Not Enemies 53
5. Environment: The Hidden Lever 67
6. The Spiral 91
7. Building Your Pressure Code 103
8. Longevity and Legacy 123
9. The Room Decides 139

Conclusion 159

Appendices—The Performance OS Field Notes 163

Appendix I—The Tools 165

Appendix II—The Principles Behind the Practice 203

Appendix III—The Notes 225

Acknowledgments 235

Notes 239

Foreword

I'm not someone who likes to explain everything.

I just pay attention to what works.

In tennis, a lot of people have opinions. A lot of people have plans. Teams change fast. Coaches come and go. That's just how it is. What matters to me is who's still there when things aren't working—when you're losing, when you're tired, when the pressure is loud and you don't really feel like talking.

Jason has been there the longest. That's not normal in this sport. And it didn't happen because everything was easy. It happened because when things were messy, we dealt with them. We talked. We argued sometimes. We figured things out and moved on. That mattered more to me than any perfect plan.

Jason says I have a lot of fire. Everyone knows that. Early on, I thought fighting harder was the answer to everything. Sometimes it was. A lot of times, it wasn't. I didn't need someone to calm me down or change who I was. I needed someone who could help me handle pressure without turning it into a bigger problem than it already was.

That's what Jason does for me.

We don't make things dramatic. We don't overthink everything. If something isn't working, we look at it and deal with it. If I'm struggling, I can say it. If I'm angry, that's fine too. Then we move forward. Simple, but not easy.

We started with a question: *Can I do this?* That belief became *How do I do this?* So we worked on specific skills. Today, it's about a new skill: *How do we stay here?* It began with me being true to myself and my values. Jason taught me how to manage my mind. Both on and off the court.

People sometimes see us before matches and laugh. There are traditions. Some of them are kind of silly. We keep them anyway. It's not magic. It's just our way of keeping things normal when everything around you is trying to make the moment feel huge. Pressure is already there. You don't need to add more.

I'm not perfect. I still lose. I still get upset. I still have days when I feel like I should have done things differently. But I'm in a better place now than I was years ago, and that didn't happen by accident. It came from building an environment I trust. From working with people who don't panic when things get uncomfortable.

This book comes from that world. It's not theory to me. It's real life. It's how things actually work when you're under pressure and there's nowhere to hide. If you're curious about that—about what it looks like up close—you can step in and see for yourself.

That's where Jason lives. And not many people get to see it up close.

—Aryna Sabalenka

INTRODUCTION

In September 2025, following Aryna Sabalenka's victory at the US Open, we found ourselves at the vibrant after party, where champagne flowed freely and a crowd of sponsors and influential people mingled. I was waiting for Aryna to finish her media rounds, sitting where I could keep an eye on her trophy, the polished metal twinkling in the low light. In the reflection, I spotted two men I'd met earlier approaching me.

I'd had a casual conversation with them—maybe three minutes, no big deal—walking them through my concept of the Performance Operating System (OS) as a way of framing elite performance. I explained that I was writing a book about how the various programs and systems people follow are like apps on a phone: They can be helpful, and it's easy to keep adding new ones, but if the underlying operating system isn't updated and clean, the apps won't work. It doesn't matter how good or how new they are. If the operating system isn't running smoothly, those apps are nothing more than a collection of pixels.

All that code is what I call the Pressure Code. Not only because it works like an operating system, but because it's a way of harmonizing and aligning your life. Like living by a warrior's code, only aimed at performance.

Anyway, that was it—I didn't go too deep. I threw out a few examples, and we shook hands before they went on their way. But now they were zeroing in on me from across the room, making a beeline for my direction.

When they reached my table, the first man looked me in the eye and exclaimed, "I need to tell you something! This has been an incredible night—we've been hanging out with Djokovic! We got to watch the final! And now we're at the after party for a US Open champion." Then he leaned in and continued under his breath, "But the only thing we've been able to think about is our conversation from earlier."

Our conversation from earlier . . . ? I didn't know what to say. I had probably spent less than five minutes with the two of them.

"We've been talking about it nonstop," the other guy jumped in. "Like all the stuff we could have influence over, and everything we're blind to that influences us. First thing tomorrow, we're going to start digging into it and auditing our systems. So when you finish that book, let us know!"

That moment really stuck with me. Not because of the compliment—though I appreciated it—but because of what it revealed. These weren't tennis people or athletes. They were billionaires, high-level finance guys, who were extremely well-connected. And yet something about our brief conversation had cut through all the noise and excitement that night for them.

Which brings me to the reason I wrote this book.

Here's the secret to performance: When the pressure spikes, we don't *rise* to the occasion. Instead, we *fall back* to the level of our code.

It's that simple. And yet, most elite performers don't want to believe it—they've been taught that they'll find another gear in the heat of the moment, summon more courage, more grit, or more willpower. But what's really happening, especially when the pressure hits, is they default back to whatever code they're running. And you, me, and everyone else are doing the same.

We all have an OS running, like it or not. And if you don't pay attention to it, like every other OS you've ever had on your phone or your computer, it's going to slow down, break down, and leave you wondering why things stopped working. You might try installing a new "app," hoping it's the key to fixing things. That "app" could be a book, a class, a coach, etc. All is fine *if* your operating system is running smoothly. But what if it's not?

You can't just think of your Pressure Code as something idling in the background. You must assess and manage it with intentionality, purpose, and a brutal level of honesty. Anything short of that will set the ceiling on your performance lower than you'd like—and that's the difference between champions and everyone else.

Where did I learn all this? Not sitting in a classroom. I learned it on the streets at 13 years old, where running an out-of-date OS meant getting hurt. Then, as a lifelong athlete, I learned it on various jiujitsu mats and in dojos, where you have to channel your emotions, stay disciplined and present, and keep your code running or you'll get choked out (and maybe black out).

I've spent several decades refining this strategic approach and then proving that the Pressure Code works with world-class athletes, Olympic teams, executives of billion-dollar companies, and people from all backgrounds seeking to improve their performance under pressure. But don't think of it as a shortcut. Productivity hacks may feel good in the short term, promising an edge, but they never hold. When the real pressure mounts, when you're chasing the same prize as all the top competitors in your field, you will default to whatever code is running beneath that "app" you installed.

Your Pressure Code is that hidden system orchestrating and enabling everything you do. It is the interplay of the 3Es: your energy, emotions, and environment.

Energy: how you build, protect, and spend your fuel
Emotions: the signals you read and how you regulate under pressure
Environment: the external and internal settings you live inside

Align them, and you create rhythm, clarity, and resilience. When this happens, you'll spiral up. Ignore them, and you'll invite noise, chaos, and confusion, inevitably spiraling down.

There's a good chance that if you're reading this book, you're familiar with the remarkable journey of Aryna Sabalenka—one of the most powerful tennis champions to ever play the game. As her performance coach, I knew that her fire made her a dangerous competitor. But it also led her to break down in critical moments.

So, to protect her from this vulnerability, Aryna's team and I worked on upgrading her code. By mid-2025, she'd won three Grand Slams over the previous two years. She was making finals and was the most consistent player on tour. But when the pressure of that time in her career reached its peak, Aryna couldn't keep it up. In the Australian Open final against Madison Keys, she smashed her racket. In the French Open final against Coco Gauff, she lost confidence in herself. In the Wimbledon semifinal, she confessed to a "hate relationship" with the whole tournament.

The press questioned her composure. Fans wondered if she was a fighter who burned bright, only to fade under the weight of expectation. But together, as a team, we got her code running smoothly. We helped her get into alignment when she drifted out and to stop fighting against her most challenging opponent—herself.

In September 2025, at Arthur Ashe Stadium in New York, Aryna defended her US Open crown with rhythm, composure, and purpose. In a historic victory, she became the first woman since Serena Williams to win back-to-back titles in New York. Most assumed she simply rose to the occasion. I knew the difference. Absolutely, she put on a display of extraordinary talent and played like the champion that she is. But that was because her code had been fine-tuned and balanced until it was running in harmony, and that made everything else possible.

If you're reading this book, there's likely a performance level you're reaching for. Maybe you're an executive who can't seem to turn off—you're grinding through back-to-back meetings, draining energy into arguments that don't matter, and snapping at the people you care about most. Or maybe you're an athlete who trains harder than anyone else but freezes when the lights come on. You just can't seem to win when it matters most. Perhaps you're a parent trying to show up with clarity and presence, but you keep circling the same negative patterns with your children. Or you're a coach looking to take your clients to the next level, but you're left wondering why nothing sticks.

Forget any advice that amounts to "just try harder." Whatever your performance goal, the problem isn't effort. The problem the pressure of performing in the real world has exposed is an outdated code. Resist installing that new "app" . . . you need an OS upgrade.

The good news is that this book is a manual for doing exactly that. Each chapter offers a new lens for seeing how energy, emotions, and environment interconnect and drive results.

Energy comes first: how you build it, protect it, and spend it with precision. Then, emotions: how to read, regulate, and process yours correctly. And finally, environment: both external (the rooms you walk into) and internal (the stories you tell yourself). Along the way, you'll see how these three elements work together to move you into a spiral—either upward into flow and trust, or downward into chaos and eventual collapse. You'll meet others who upgraded their operating systems and changed their lives. You'll learn how to build a Performance OS that actually holds steady when life hits hard. By the end, you'll know how to audit your own system, identify where it's leaking, and patch the code that runs beneath everything you do.

I'll start by sharing my own survival story. Then we'll follow Aryna's transformation from raw fire and talent to finely tuned champion, operating on an elite level.

A FINAL NOTE

You should revisit this book often. Maybe you'll read something that impacts you, but then life will get loud, and you'll lose the thread, forget the lesson, or react the way you swore you wouldn't. That's when you need to pick the book up again and employ the tools and strategies to patch a fix. The Pressure Code isn't a one-and-done idea that lives on your shelf. It's a framework that's always running as you live your life. And how you experience that life—whether intentionally or at the default set by your unattended code—is up to you.

Let me use a climbing metaphor to offer another perspective on this. Each chapter focuses entirely on the ascent. Each step takes you further along the upward spiral. That climb—whether on the court, in the dojo, in the boardroom, or at home—will bring pressure. I'll show you how the system functions when it's working and the costs involved when it breaks. Consider the appendices your base camp—use them to recover, study, relearn, and rebuild. Each offers a tool for your toolkit. Some are highly specialized, while others overlap. The key is to choose the one that best serves you when you need it. You'll find them organized into three categories:

- *Appendix I—The Tools:* Practical aids and tools to employ to audit, check in, and reset.
- *Appendix II—The Principles Behind the Practice:* Go deeper into the philosophical glue that holds the OS together.
- *Appendix III—The Notes:* Reflections and letters that serve as quick reminders and checkpoints that catch you when you're feeling the pressure.

In the first chapter, I'll start by sharing my story of childhood tragedy. You'll learn how I personally came face-to-face with the brutality of the world. I take pride in my unique story, and it's important background info for appreciating how my approach is different from the other models out there. To understand where we're headed, we must start at the beginning. It wasn't a path I would wish on anyone, but through it, I found peace, family, and the performance edge.

Remember, pressure is a privilege. When the real world pushes against our code, that's our catalyst for growth. The goal isn't to resist it; it's to catch it and turn it into fuel. And that's what the Pressure Code is all about—turning pressure into a beautiful thing.

So, if you're ready, let's go!

Chapter One

FROM FIGHTER TO WARRIOR

I was 13 when I became homeless. People often ask me how that happened. It's not the kind of story you expect to become *your* story.

When I was younger, my dad was in the Air Force. One of my clearest memories is of being in the garage with him at the base, climbing around on this giant truck while he was working. The smell of oil and metal still takes me right back.

One day, my dad told me about a coworker who got caught with drugs on the premises. The man was about to lose his career and family—basically everything. I remember he looked at me and said, "Jason, stay away from this at any cost."

That moment burned itself into my memory, and I took his advice to heart.

Later, my dad was in a serious motorcycle accident. At first, I thought maybe we'd gotten lucky; that he'd dodged the worst of it. But one morning, it all turned. Suddenly, my mom was on the phone, desperately talking with paramedics. She was in full panic mode as she tried to follow their instructions. I was told it was my job to keep my dad awake. Keeping him awake meant keeping him breathing and alive until the paramedics got there.

So, I tried.

I shook him. I begged him. But my dad's eyes kept rolling back.

When help came, they worked on him right in front of me—but it was too late. I watched as they silently lifted him into the ambulance. No one had to say a thing. I knew. I saw it in their movements. I saw it in the look on my mom's face. It was over.

That day broke everything about my life and shattered my mom. She had to find work. Then she got injured, so it all got harder after that. I was 11 years old. I got myself a paper route to bring in extra money. I stepped up to take care of my little brother and sister, getting them ready in the mornings, walking them to school, and making sure they ate.

I tried to be there for them as best I could, but I was just a kid myself. And despite my best efforts, nothing could change the fact that the center of gravity in our home had disappeared the day my dad died. And with it, our house had stopped feeling like a home.

One night, we left everything behind and flew to another state to start over. But things got even worse. I took a job living with a family and watching their kids, but that family had its own demons. Eventually, my mom and siblings returned to our previous home—or so I thought. When I went back, the house was empty. With no internet or cell phones, I had no idea where they had gone or how to find them. Standing alone in that empty house, I made a decision: Wherever they were, they were better off without me. One less mouth to feed. I'd survive on my own.

I ended up on the streets, surrounded by drugs and violence. I lost friends. I saw things no one should ever see, let alone a child. Yet, through all of that, I never forgot what my dad had told me. Even when refusing drugs meant getting hurt, I stayed away from them. That decision saved my life.

THE ENVIRONMENT THAT SHAPES YOU

Being homeless in the early nineties was an unforgiving experience.

Sirens split the nights. Storefront windows wore bars like armor, and the corners belonged to the gangs. Violence was constant. Two of my friends committed suicide in front of me. I experienced death, up close and personal.

I carried everything I owned in a beat-up backpack. It was littered with small holes that I'd patched up with duct tape to keep the roaches out. The backpack was easier to travel with, but when I needed to hide my belongings, I used a small box and stashed it behind a dumpster. Pack or box, my entire life fit in one container.

Sleep was never really sleep. Some nights, I curled against the back of a building, using my jacket as a makeshift pillow, attempting to make myself as small as possible. But I had to be alert, even in sleep. A car door would slam, jolting me awake. If footsteps sounded too close, my whole body would go rigid, preparing for the worst. People would attack me in my sleep, often high and freaking out. Sometimes, they thought I was a narc or an enemy because I wouldn't get involved with the drug scene.

The cold cut through my thin layers of clothing, but worse still was the hunger. I'd linger outside of bakeries just to breathe in the smell of fresh bread. I'd grab whatever scraps I could out of the trash. Some days, if I was lucky, a festival or some other event would leave behind scraps I could salvage. Sometimes, there was nothing to eat, and I was forced to just keep walking. To keep moving.

Living on the streets in a constant fight for survival taught me a fundamental truth: Your environment doesn't just surround you; it programs you. It teaches your body and mind what's possible, what's dangerous, and what's normal. I was programmed by my environment to believe that violence was random and trust was costly. I learned that survival meant staying hyper-alert, reading every signal, and making myself small enough to be overlooked but sharp enough to never be caught off guard. At first, I believed fighting was the only way to survive. Later, I would learn the difference between being a fighter—merely surviving—and being a warrior.

THE LIFE OF A FIGHTER

Being a fighter isn't about how well you can throw a punch. It's about noting the way someone's shoulders tighten before they swing. It's about the eyes, and how well you can read a room. Catching the way a laugh turns sharp right before it becomes dangerous. When you see a man crumpled in the shadows, can you tell if he's a harmless drunk or a predator waiting for a victim? You have seconds to choose, and your life depends on it.

On the streets, eye contact is a language with consequences. Stare too long, and you issue a challenge. Look away too fast, and you signal fear. Both can get you hurt. I learned to read a room in a fraction of a second and adjust my behavior accordingly. Often, I had to make myself small, shoulders in and eyes down, just enough to seem invisible. Other times, I went neutral—present but not threatening, just another body moving through the crowd. And sometimes, I had to stand up straight, shoulders back, and lock eyes. No flinching. No blinking. Because in that moment, showing fear meant giving them permission to act on it.

Your fluency in this language will rise under pressure. I once got smashed in the head with a gun, followed by the barrel pressed against my temple. My life hung in the balance of that moment, waiting to be determined by how I would react. Despite the adrenaline flooding my veins and my heart racing frantically, I stood still. I didn't move a muscle; I didn't look away. I just stood there.

The man holding the gun was testing me. Waiting for me to

flinch, to beg, to break. But I didn't give him anything. You learn fast in moments like that: Your body is the only message that you have, and you have to control it. Being a fighter means running on nerves stretched tight and reading people like your life depends on it—because it just might.

Fighting is never really a solo endeavor. On the streets, it was always tribe against tribe—"your" people against "theirs." You learn quickly where you stand and who you stand with. But even among your tribe, loyalty is a fragile thing. Fighters don't have the luxury of building authentic trust, and they spend it recklessly because they know they aren't guaranteed to see another dawn.

Being a fighter isn't about winning. Fighters simply survive.

This was my world as a teenager: the streets, the violence, the hunger. Survival. I was just trying to make it through one more night and see the sunrise one more time. My days were a combination of clenched fists and fast feet—always on edge.

My environment made me a fighter. And if that world was all I had ever known, it's all I would have become. Luckily, I discovered two places that made me something more.

REFUGE

The first saving environment I found was the library. Walking through those doors, I left the violence of the streets behind and crossed into another world—one with warm air, steady light, and the comforting smell of worn leather and paper. I'd head into the bathroom first to wash my face and my hands and try to look like someone who belonged in a place like this. Then I'd drink from the water fountains until my stomach stopped cramping.

The librarian never asked questions, never wondered why I was there. She just quietly stamped my card and allowed me to stay. I'd disappear between the shelves, losing myself in the books for hours. I pored over newspapers on film reels and flipped through martial arts manuals, trying to piece together the world I wanted to live in. The books carried me farther than my feet ever could. They brought me to places beyond dark alleyways and bus stops, where danger wasn't a constant, and horizons were broad, where kids like me weren't invisible.

I treasured the precious hours of comfortable quiet that I spent in the library, where I didn't have to brace for every sound. That silence was a mercy.

My second refuge was the dojo. It was wedged between a pawnshop and an adult bookstore—not exactly the type of place you'd expect a kid to find salvation. But day after day, I'd press my face against the glass and watch what was happening inside.

Eventually, I worked up the courage to sneak in. The smell of mats and sweat greeted me as I slipped through the door. The snap of a Gi collar broke up the sounds of people training, their bodies covered in bruises as proof of their hard work and learning. I watched as they bowed at the door to enter and bowed to their partner. They looked everyone in the eyes. Not as a challenge or a threat but simply to show respect. Respect was required.

Eventually, I was invited to stay. The head sensei and one of his black belts allowed me to just sit and watch the classes for a while. Then, they took me to the back office and asked about me and my situation. I shared my story, and they must have seen something in me. Or rather, they saw *me*. I wasn't just the homeless kid you avoided eye contact with as you walked down the street—I was a whole person. And, despite being without parents to sign the forms, they let me stay—a lifeline. And never charged me a dime.

In the dojo, I learned more than how to fight. I learned discipline. I learned respect. I learned that I could belong somewhere. I will never forget the words my sensei, Jan Sunderlin, once told me: "Through loyalty, you gain trust. With trust comes freedom. To maintain that freedom, remain loyal." As a kid, I couldn't yet understand the depth of his words—on the streets, trust was just another currency. But I could feel the weight behind what he'd said. I knew he meant it. And for a kid raised on broken promises, that stability was everything.

The dojo was where my understanding of fighting shifted. On the street, every move was motivated by fear and adrenaline, powered by feral desperation. In the dojo, every strike carried form, timing, and purpose. Where the street demanded reaction, the dojo required discipline.

As I trained, I learned that fear and adrenaline don't make you strong—they make you reckless and rob you of control. Most importantly, I learned that surviving one night isn't the same as living with purpose. That's where the true shift began.

FROM FIGHTER TO WARRIOR

While fighting had kept me breathing, becoming a warrior gave me direction, and martial arts gave me the language to process this shift:

- *Zanshin*—remaining mind. Calm awareness after the strike. Steady and ready for what's next.
- *Mushin*—no mind. Flow without clutter. Action without hesitation.
- *Tomaranu kokoro*—indomitable spirit. The decision to hold your values even when it costs you everything. That one nearly got me killed more than once. But I knew if I bent, I'd lose more than a fight—I'd lose myself.

This shift from fighter to warrior is relevant in any context and to everyone who steps into the arena of life. Whether that's on the court or in the boardroom, the goal is to move beyond a state of constant fighting.

Fighters burn out, but warriors endure.

Fighters react, but warriors choose.

Fighters are driven by chaos, but warriors carry discipline.

Fighters fight for the moment, but warriors fight for something bigger.

Warriors build a system. The code is more than a philosophy; it's a compass for performance, for coaching, and for life. It's a pressure code—the same rules that kept me alive in the chaos of the streets are the ones that keep athletes, leaders, and parents steady when the pressure ramps up. When I was younger, I didn't have a language for what I was learning. But the code was already being written.

DEFINING THE CODE

Your code is born from your values. For me, those foundational values are presence, loyalty, discipline, awareness, adaptability, courage, and stillness.

As I walk you through each of my values, I'm not suggesting they are the "right" ones. Everyone will have their own set from which their Pressure Code will operate. But because achieving high performance requires a brutal level of honesty, you'll need to be grounded in your values first. Otherwise, the temptation for shortcuts and hacks can be too enticing.

My own values started with presence. When you don't know where your next meal's coming from, you either live in the moment or you don't make it. Fighters may drift into the past or the future; warriors stay right where their feet are, firmly rooted in the present. That's what lets them anticipate the next move before it happens. It's what lets them breathe before they speak, adjust before they break.

Then came loyalty. On the streets, loyalty means survival. In leadership, it means consistency—the kind of reliability people can feel. Loyalty builds trust, and trust is the chemistry that binds teams into a cohesive unit, keeping them from fracturing under pressure.

And then there's discipline. Discipline isn't about punishment; it's about alignment. It means bowing at the door even when nobody is watching. Showing respect, even when every part of you is threatening to snap. Doing what the moment demands, not what emotion wants. I learned early on that something as simple as two slow breaths in the heat of the moment can save you hours of damage control later.

Awareness followed. In the dojo, we call it *zanshin*—remaining mind. The fight isn't over when the punch lands; it's over when you're calm enough to see what comes next. That awareness has become a constant thread in everything I do. Whether it's a championship match or a conversation with my kids, awareness is what keeps me neutral—engaged, but not tangled up in my emotions.

From there, adaptability. *Mushin*—no mind. Flow without friction. When you've reached a certain level of training, you stop craving control. You learn to let the system take over. That's what frees up an elite performer to pivot mid-play, or a leader to shift tone mid-meeting without losing composure. Control is brittle; clarity is fluid.

Courage ties all the other values together. Courage is not the absence of fear, but the conscious choice to take action despite it. Every major step in my life—from walking into that first dojo to coaching on the biggest stages—was some version of the same moment. I felt the fear, and I took action anyway.

And finally, stillness—maybe the hardest lesson for me to learn. For a fighter, rest feels like a collapse. For a warrior, it feels like recalibration. Stillness is the reset that makes your next action cleaner and sharper than it was before. When you're younger, it's easy to conflate momentum with strength. Later, I realized that the power is in the *rhythm*.

That's the Pressure Code I strive to live by—the state of coherence while taking action directed by and aligned to my values: Presence. Loyalty. Discipline. Awareness. Adaptability. Courage. Stillness.

Defining your values builds the foundation that will influence your greatest aspirations and determine your reactions along the way. But it's not easy. You don't master them all at once, and you won't always start with the one you resist most. As you assess what's working and what's not—from resources, to people, to skills and attitudes—you'll take all the good with all the bad, and start prioritizing where to focus your attention. It starts with several small steps, but your priority should always be the thing you can take action on *now*. Once you get the system moving, the pieces will come together. And as they do, you'll begin to see the various connections and opportunities for even more improvement—upgrading your OS. Starting is the key.

ARYNA'S BREAKTHROUGH

As a coach, I see that code playing out every season on tour. The arenas change, and the lights get brighter, but the battle is always the same. It's always between rhythm and reaction, control and trust.

A few summers ago, I watched this struggle unfold in real time with Aryna. From the outside, she was flying—titles, sponsorships, headlines. But beneath the surface, the system was straining. Aryna's intensity fills the court, and the fans love the chaos. Commentators have called her fearless. But that level of intensity won't carry you through the hardest matches—not at her level. When you're at the pinnacle of a sport, any tiny crack will show.

In January 2025, Aryna was at the Australian Open as the reigning two-time champion and the heavy favorite. She was in Melbourne to defend her title for a potentially historic third year in a row. But in the final against Madison Keys, the nerves hit. She dropped the first set. Clawed back the second. And in the decider, her fire turned wild. She smashed her racket in frustration before shaking hands. And the cameras caught it all.

Headlines didn't miss their chance: "Sabalenka loses her cool in Australian Open collapse."

Then came Paris. It was the French Open final, center court across from Coco Gauff. Aryna took the first set in a tie-break. The title was right there! But her rhythm slipped. Errors piled up. She lost 6-7, 6-2, 6-4. Later, she admitted what the world could already see: She didn't fully trust herself.

At Wimbledon, it was déjà vu. She fought through to the semifinal but ultimately lost to Amanda Anisimova in three sets. Another deep run, another heartbreak. In the press room afterward, she confessed to reporters, "Losing sucks . . . you feel like you want to die. You don't want to exist anymore. I have a hate relationship with Wimbledon." Outside the Slams, the pattern held. In Dubai, she fell to a much lower-ranked player. She knew emotionally she was not at her best.

Earlier, when her serve was falling apart, week after week, tournament after tournament, she'd show up, fight through matches, and lose the same way: double faults at the worst times. Her confidence was draining with every loss. Fighting had been her identity—prove you're tougher, outlast everyone, grind your way through. But grit without the rhythm to support it will break you.

So, we worked on her Pressure Code, engineering the delicate interplay between the 3Es, energy, emotions, and environment. It would have been easy to run to a new "app" in the hunt to turn things around. But to her credit, Aryna resisted that temptation. Instead, we were able to coach her back into harmony.

The Ribeiro brothers, legends in Brazilian jiujitsu, have a

principle called Flow Pressure Finish. It is the art of presence over brute force as the combatant applies steady pressure—never frantic, but also never absent. They stay close enough to feel the other person's rhythm, but not so close they lose their own. This is the paradox of control through calm.

The same principle applies under the tournament lights. Performance is the art of constant engagement under pressure. Like *zanshin*, it requires the posture of someone who sees everything without grasping at it: calm without passivity, aggression without recklessness. Aryna learned how to live there again, once she stopped chasing control and started creating it, and the OS harmonized.

Next, Arthur Ashe Stadium. September 2025. New York. Across the net stood Amanda Anisimova, the same player who had beaten Aryna at Wimbledon months before. The crowd leaned in, remembering her breakdowns, wondering if the cycle would repeat.

But this was a different Aryna.

She didn't rush. She didn't spiral. Instead, she played with rhythm, with purpose. She had fewer unforced errors, and in the second-set tie-break, she maintained her composure. She won 6-3, 7-6(3), defending her US Open crown and becoming the first woman since Serena Williams to go back-to-back in New York.

In the press conferences after the win, the reporters asked about me, about my background, my homelessness, my martial arts training, and my fighter mentality. They wanted to know how much I'd helped influence her, how much I'd taught her about fighting, about grit, about never giving up.

Her answer stopped me in my tracks: "Jason helped me understand what real fighting is, what fighting really means."

Winning is not about grinding or endless emotional battles. It's not achieved by the pure fuel-and-fire approach that burns hot and fades fast. Like Aryna said, I taught her the difference between being a fighter and being a warrior. And as a warrior, she could manage the difficult challenges that grinding alone can't overcome.

Fighters hope; warriors prepare. And in that moment, she proved she'd made the shift.

THE EVERYDAY FIGHTER

Not every fighter fights under stadium lights. I worked with a leader who looked like he was succeeding on the outside but was actually living the same way I had at 13: hyper-alert, braced for impact every day, and grinding himself into exhaustion just to survive. Back-to-back meetings. Late nights on email. A grueling travel schedule that left no time for him to recover. He carried stress in his shoulders, in his jaw, in the way he snapped at his team without meaning to. And at home, the same weight spilled over. His body was breaking down. His relationships were frayed. In life as in work, he had stopped leading and instead was merely reacting.

That's what a fighter looks like—in a suit.

When we started working together, he just wanted an easy hack, another productivity app that promised a better way to manage stress. But that wasn't what he needed. So instead, we mapped his Pressure Code, just like I had with Aryna. Where was his energy being created, and what was draining it? What environments fueled him, and which ones were holding him back? What emotions was he running from instead of regulating?

Slowly, the shift began.

He stopped treating rest like a weakness. He began shaping his days instead of letting them shape him. Found rhythm instead of running on fumes. And the people around him noticed. Meetings that used to spiral turned into decisions with clear outcomes. His team leaned in instead of backing away. His family discovered a man who was present, not just exhausted.

The relief on his face when it clicked—that he didn't have to keep fighting every minute—that was the same relief I'd seen in Aryna. And it was the same relief I'd felt in the dojo all those years ago.

The pressure we face doesn't care who you are; it only cares how your code is built. But the surprising thing is that pressure can be a beautiful thing. In the pages ahead, we'll lay out the fuel that moves you, the signals that keep you honest, and the conditions that steady you. Then, it's your job to train your OS until it lives in your bones.

Your story lives in the past.

Your system lives in the now.

What you do with that system next will determine your future.

So, let's start installing the code.

Chapter Two

THE SWEET SPOT OF PERFORMANCE

During a tennis match, while others are paying attention to the ball, the serve, the return, or the rally, I'm watching what happens *in between* the points. I watch Aryna's shoulders. Her breath. The way she walks back to the baseline. How she holds her racket. Whether her eyes are on the strings or scanning the crowd.

When Aryna had stepped onto the clay at Roland-Garros in June 2025, she initially looked ready. In the French Open final, she took the first set against Coco Gauff in a tense tie-break. The power was there. The precision was there. But under pressure, something inside her cracked. Her shoulders sagged. Her errors multiplied. And where Gauff remained steady, Aryna unraveled. What started as a contest turned into a spiral. She lost 6-7(5), 6-2, 6-4. Her system collapsed under the pressure.

Being a fighter feels noble. You show up, you take the hits, and you push harder. But as a warrior, your goal is to win the war. That means facing your fears and pausing long enough to ask the tough questions. You know the ones—they're the questions you'd rather avoid. And yet, engaging with them is the only way to find what I call the sweet spot.

THE MAGNIFYING GLASS

Even with all her raw power, Aryna still lost the Australian Open. And it was the way she lost that proved her failure was driven by more than a bad day or a swing gone wrong. She had had the chance to make history: two straight titles and a 20-match win streak at Melbourne Park were at stake. The court was familiar, but the goals were ambitious, and the expectations were heavy.

Against Madison Keys, she slipped. Aryna lost 6-3, 2-6, 7-5. Keys found shot after shot as Aryna's errors piled up. The crowd held its breath as the final set tightened, but Aryna's frustration told the story before the scoreboard did. When it ended, she smashed her racket, pulled a towel over her head, and walked off before the trophy ceremony began.

That match was a mirror. Her energy had drained early. Her emotions had controlled her choices. The crowd noise, the pressure, and the expectations of her environment had tightened and suffocated her instead of providing support. And the mirror's reflection showed a life out of balance. If one of the 3Es is off, it pulls the others down.

The match was also a magnifying glass. Losses like that reveal where the Pressure Code is lacking, when the cracks are too hard to see unaided. In Aryna's case, we were able to use these magnified truths as a learning opportunity. We audited her energy cycles, her mental resets, and the environment she occupied before stepping on the court. The pressure revealed her faulty code. Next, it was our job to rewrite it.

WHEN EMOTION HIJACKS EVERYTHING

A few months later in Paris, it was the same story. Grand Slam final. Clay courts. Pressure. Expectations. Aryna took the first set in a tie-break. She looked composed. Her serves were smart, and she struck hard. But then the wind turned. Her mistakes piled up, and her composure faltered. Unforced misses. Mental lapses. Moments where she rushed instead of resetting.

Gauff turned it around, winning 6-7(5), 6-2, 6-4. That loss cut deeper than any single point. All Aryna's raw power and physical prep weren't enough. When her emotion spiked, it nuked her rhythm. Like all of us, when her internal environment was unsteady, the external noise got even louder.

What was missing in her OS? What did the pressure reveal in her code? It revealed that she didn't trust herself. She wasn't resetting mentally. She let her emotions run away, resulting in unforced errors. Her environment was draining her instead of supporting her.

Aryna's losses mattered as much as her wins. They lit up the shadowed parts of her system and exposed the cracks. We looked hard at her energy cycles. What emotional triggers threw her off? What environmental factors—wind, crowd, conditions, people, conversations, outside activities, events, and, of course, expectations—had she been unprepared for? Then, we went back to work.

GETTING BEYOND THE BREAKDOWN

At Aryna's level, it's expected she'll make finals, that she'll be competitive, and more often than not, that she'll win. That's a lot of pressure, especially in tennis, which is a year-round sport with no off-season. There's a lot of uncertainty—you don't even know who you're playing until the night before. Add to that lots of international travel and all the points you have to manage. It's no easy feat.

But elite performance is always achieved systemically. It's never the result of a single isolated factor. You don't win because you're confident, or disciplined, or passionate. You win because you've learned to regulate and align the core systems that control everything else.

You likely have all kinds of apps on your phone right now: sleep trackers, media players, productivity helpers, coaching platforms. But without a functioning OS, they're useless. I've coached jiujitsu fighters who perform at an elite level in the dojo during training. Flawless technique. Consistent wins. Dominant on the mat. But the moment they step into competition, they fall apart.

Why? Was their jiujitsu "app" suddenly broken? No, their system failed. Maybe they didn't manage the environmental shift from practice to the public arena—expectations, crowd, judges, unfamiliar stimuli adding pressure. Maybe they didn't manage their energy profile—overtraining the week prior, under-recovering, warming up with too much intensity, failing to calibrate arousal levels. Emotionally? Maybe they hesitated, overthought, tightened up. Their fight-or-flight system hijacked the body. Their breath shortened. Their focus narrowed to the wrong target.

I watched them lose, not because the jiujitsu "app" stopped working but because the pressure of competition revealed the cracks in their OS. They fell to the level of their code. It's a breakdown that happens every day. Boardrooms. Bullpens. Sales calls. Startup pitches. Parenting. Teaching. Trading. Writing. Speaking. Coaching. Your technique "app" without a system will always be fragile. Pressure will break it every time—which is why assessing and aligning the 3Es is the key to strengthening your Pressure Code. Why the 3Es?

Energy is your currency. It's created, protected, and spent with intention. But if you burn it faster than you build it, nothing else will matter. All your training and preparation will mean nothing if you don't have the energy when the moment comes.

Emotions are signals to read and regulate, not enemies to suppress. If you ignore them, they will hijack your body and mind. But if you learn to use them, they sharpen you.

Environment is more than the space around you. It's the conditions you live in, both external and internal. A poorly shaped environment pulls you down. A well-shaped one lifts you up.

THE SWEET SPOT

It's easy to believe performance comes down to one moment. One shot. One mistake. The serve that double faults. The forehand that sails long. That's what the highlight reels show—the visible errors, the flashpoints. But the truth is different. Matches are rarely won or lost on a single stroke. They're won in the spaces between—where nobody is looking or managing—in the harmony and flow of the operating system at work.

The sweet spot is where your operating system has found balance and harmony between the 3Es. When your 3Es are aligned, when you're aware of and working through the layers of the system, pressure is no longer a resistance, but a fuel. It's a force that you get to choose to apply to your opponent, your life, and the various obstacles and opportunities you're confronted with. The sweet spot is where pressure becomes power, fueled by a sense of control, clarity, and alignment. It creates coherence.

Physiologically, coherence is the balance between your sympathetic and parasympathetic systems. It happens when your breath, heart, and mind are playing at the same tempo, your system is no longer fighting against itself, and you're in a state of controlled flow. You'll know you're there when there's a stretch of time that everything just *works*. You're not thinking. You're not checking the clock. You're in it—body, breath, and everything else lined up like it was meant to be there all along.

People often treat it like a ghost story. They talk about it in whispers—some lucky break, a rare high that can't be repeated. Not true. I've watched it happen too many times to call it luck. You feel it in the body first—the air gets heavy, the sound sharpens, colors stretch a little wider. You could swear you can hear your own pulse syncing with the room. Your internal energy, emotions, and environment are all pulling the same way and lining up.

Elite performance isn't about peak moments. Rather, it's about shortening the distance between chaos and control. When you understand what your version of the sweet spot feels like—its temperature, its sound, its rhythm—you stop chasing it like luck. You start running your Pressure Code, one cycle at a time, on a continuous loop, knowing that as you ascend, you'll eventually find it.

THE OS LOOP

When I start working with a new athlete or leader, I don't begin with mindset or mechanics. I start by teaching them how to loop their system. Each day, their bodies and brains are gathering data—breath, posture, tone, focus, the feel of the room, etc. Most of the time, they ignore it until something breaks. Looping is the way to stay ahead of that break.

NOTICE

It starts with paying attention and noticing what's happening with and around you. No labels or judgments, just awareness. The small signals always show up first: shoulders tight before a meeting, restless scrolling before bed, the edge that creeps into your voice when you're tired. Those are the tells that one of your 3Es is out of sync. Catch them early, and you stay in control. Miss them, and you end up chasing recovery after the fact.

MAP

Once you notice something's off, map it. That means working through the *what*, *who*, *how*, and *when* based on what you can control. I'll ask a client where they feel it. If it's energy, we talk about sleep, fuel, and the pace they're running. If it's emotions, we use a short reset—drop the shoulders back, open the chest, and make space. Breathe twice, set posture, aim attention. If it's their environment, we change something physical. Move to another space. Clear the noise. Adjust the lighting. It's also mapping the people who are showing up. Who has access to your environment, and how do they interact with you and others? Some people will offer a strong, safe, and supportive presence. Others will need attention, or drain your energy, or come in with emotions that are off (either too much or too little).

REALIGN

Next, you shift the elements you've noticed and mapped, prioritizing them based on what's needed for the challenge you're about to face. You're looking at both what you're currently doing and what you should start doing (all within your control) that aligns with the performance ahead.

APPLY

The next step is applying it by running one small correction. Most people want to overhaul everything at once, but that approach never sticks. I tell them to pick one thing—a morning routine, a nightly reset, a single breath before speaking when tension builds—and run it for a week. One update at a time is how a system learns. You're not transforming overnight; you're refining how you respond under pressure.

ASSESS

At the end of the day, close the loop by asking three questions:

- What worked?
- What needs work?
- What's next?

Write it down, because awareness fades fast when life speeds up. The next morning, that small review becomes the start of the next loop. This cycle is how you build consistency back in. Quietly, over time, by paying attention and noticing, mapping, realigning, applying, and assessing at the end of the day. Do it consistently enough, and it will become natural.

GETTING CONSISTENT

Consistency is a rhythm. Running the loop trains you to sense the small signals of precipitation before they turn into full storms. And that's the real work: catching tension when it's a whisper and not a crisis. And you'll discover pressure isn't something to escape, but a force you can shape.

People talk about flow in almost mystical terms, as if it's only bestowed on the most gifted. But finding the sweet spot isn't about magic. It's about cultivating coherence. You've experienced this phenomenon before but likely lacked the language to describe it. That run where time folded in on itself because you felt so in tune with your body. That meeting where words landed before you thought them. That conversation where silence did most of the talking.

The loop is how you build to the sweet spot. But you can't stay there forever. You move in and out of it, adjusting as the conditions shift. Then, flow will stop being a kind of miraculous reward and will solidify into the result of good system design.

That's your Performance OS system at work, harmonizing the 3Es as you cycle through and continually update the code.

Chapter Three

ENERGY: THE CURRENCY OF PERFORMANCE

Aryna was playing more matches than almost anyone else on tour in 2025. In March, she made the finals at Indian Wells and won the Miami Open. After that, it was straight to Europe, where she immediately made back-to-back finals. She lost the first and won the next. She had quarterfinals the next week, and then the French Open. Five tournaments after her loss in Dubai, with four finals in a row and a quarterfinal, and she won half of them! So many matches on top of each other, across a brutal schedule. Is it any wonder she was so exhausted?

And every time she entered a draw, she had to restart the emotional cycle from scratch. Week after week, tournament after tournament. New city. New court. New opponent. New expectations. Then, win or lose, we'd hop on a plane and start all over again.

The physical toll was obvious. But what people didn't see was the mental and emotional cost of constantly restarting that engine. Every tournament demanded a full energy investment—physical, mental, and emotional. And when you don't have time in between to fully recharge, you start carrying that energy debt forward.

By the time she'd get to a Grand Slam—these massive seven-match events that demand everything from a person—she was showing up already exhausted, sometimes even sick. I'd watch her fight through the early rounds running on fumes, and somehow, she'd will herself through six matches. But by the time she hit that seventh match, the deficit would catch up.

The stressors were too much, and her resources were too depleted. We'd keep adding more load to a system that was already overdrawn. It was only a matter of time before it broke.

In one tournament, she played six matches while battling an illness. The press called it grit. I called it unsustainable. She was a fighter, grinding through on sheer willpower. But again, fighters don't have systems. They have heart, certainly. But heart only carries you so far when your body has nothing left.

That's when we had to step back and really look at what we were doing. She was playing so well that she kept advancing deep into every tournament, which sounds like a good problem to have until you realize the calendar doesn't care how tired you are. The next event starts whether you're ready or not.

We had to identify how to manage her energy better. Not just in matches and in practice, but across the entire season. We had to time her schedule differently, figuring out where we'd skip tournaments, where we'd play, and where we'd rest. The goal was simple: Find her peak at the Slams and then strategically plan her energy around it.

I see the same thing with executives walking into boardrooms already emotionally in debt. Parents sitting down to dinner, already depleted. Students staring at exams with nothing left to give. I teach them all the same lesson: Your energy is your currency. You can't wait around hoping to find it. You have to create it, protect it, and spend it on purpose.

THE ENERGY LEDGER

Every day, you're running an energy ledger. Deposits are put in, withdrawals are taken out, and the balance is carried forward. Most people walk into critical moments already overdrawn. They don't realize they've been leaking energy for hours, days, weeks. And when the moments that matter show up, they're already running on empty.

To manage your ledger, you have three moves:

- Build your reserves by creating deposits.
- Protect what you have by guarding against leaky withdrawals.
- Spend your energy wisely by investing deliberately.

Build without spending, and you become a hoarder, always training, never testing. Protect without building, and you become brittle, safe but ineffective. Spend without replenishing, and you burn out fast.

Sustainable performance comes from cycling through all three with strategic intent.

BUILD: CREATING DEPOSITS

You don't stumble into energy. You build it through intentional actions and deposits. Here are some ways you can start making deposits for yourself.

SLEEP

Every system in your body runs on sleep: your cognitive speed, memory, emotional control, hormonal balance. Miss the basics here, and nothing else matters. I've watched athletes try to train through a sleep debt. I've watched executives pound caffeine to make up for it. It never works. Your body keeps the books, and eventually it collects.

Treat bedtime like a critical business meeting. Pick a target, protect it, and hit it within a 30-minute window. This week, pick three nights to cut screen time one hour earlier. Replace it with a wind-down ritual. Stretch, read, journal. In the morning, log the difference that you feel in your energy.

BREATH

Breathing is the fastest way to change state. Faster than caffeine. Faster than pep talks. Faster than music. Breathe in through the nose. Exhale longer out through the mouth. Two cycles can ease your anxiety and shift your state from chaos to composed.

Breathing is your master switch, and it works in any context.

After Roland-Garros and then Wimbledon, Aryna came to me just before the US Open and started asking questions—not about her fitness, but about the mental and emotional side. She'd been reading, thinking, and wrestling with things she used to keep locked in her head.

That was new. She used to power through challenges silently, afraid that speaking the fear out loud would make it real or make it worse. But this time, she came forward for support.

She asked me to reteach her the breathing exercises we'd done years earlier. Not for matches—for everything. Sponsor dinners. Photo shoots. Media days. Practice breaks. Moments when the spotlight had nothing to do with tennis but still demanded her energy. So we worked on it. She started pulling the reset loop into her daily rhythm: Roll your shoulders back, open your chest, breathe in through the nose, hold for a few seconds, then even slower out through the mouth, posture reset, and then move forward.

By the time we got to the US Open, she wasn't just using breath between points. She started using it between conversations, between all her obligations, between the different versions of herself that she had to show to the world.

And that's the goal. Breathwork is more than a "sport hack." It's the operating system for pressure. Whether it's a boardroom presentation, a negotiation, or your kid melting down at dinner, two clean cycles of breath, especially one long exhale before entering a room that matters, can change your entire response.

Try using the 4/2/8 loop: Inhale for four seconds, hold for two seconds, then exhale for eight. Do it sitting in traffic, before calls, or in transition moments. Notice how quickly your nervous system steadies. The exact timing can vary based on your ability, but the focus stays the same: Sit tall, open your chest, and spend more time exhaling than inhaling. The key is the longer exhale—spending more time breathing out than breathing in helps settle the system and quiet the noise. Beyond simple inhale-exhale drills, breathwork can be trained like a muscle. Short breath holds and CO_2 tolerance drills can expand your ability to stay calm under pressure.

Here's another variation to test out: After a normal inhale, exhale fully and hold for as long as you can without straining. Do three rounds. It trains your system to stay composed when stress spikes. Integrate these drills with movement—walking or light exercise—so breath control becomes automatic.

MOVEMENT

Your body isn't a brain taxi. The way you move dictates the way you think and feel. Stuck posture equals stuck perspective.

Move before you need it. Insert one stretch break into your schedule every 90 minutes. It can be any type of movement, as long as it's two minutes—walking, stretching, shadowboxing. These small bursts of movement will compound over time. They train your nervous system to recover faster under stress.

FUEL

Food is fuel. Get it wrong, and you're on a blood-sugar rollercoaster. Get it right, and you stabilize your emotional and cognitive output. What you eat will have an instant impact on your hormonal state, both immediately and in the hours that follow. And based on how your body is responding, food is also information. It helps you perceive things more objectively and manage your emotions better.

What you eat right now will directly impact how you think, feel, and process information. Front-load protein and hydration. For one week, eat 20–30 grams of protein within an hour of waking. Carry a water bottle everywhere. Track your afternoon crash and see how it shifts.

CONNECTION

We're wired for resonance. A 30-second check-in with someone you trust can drop cortisol more effectively than another productivity hack. It's biochemical.

Quality beats quantity. Each day, pick one person. Make a genuine, undistracted connection. Look them in the eye, ask one real question, and listen. Note your energy levels and log how your body feels afterward.

Deposits aren't glamorous. They aren't the newest trending life hack, and they won't go viral. But deposits done consistently will transform your energy levels. They're the difference between stepping into the arena full or bankrupt.

PROTECT: GUARDING AGAINST LEAKY WITHDRAWALS

Most people don't lack energy. They leak it.

You can train hard, eat clean, and even sleep eight hours every night, but if your system is riddled with leaks, you'll stay bankrupt. The danger of leaks is that they're subtle—you don't notice how much energy you're leaking until it's too late. Nobody notices the small drains that accumulate throughout the day, the pointless conversations, unproductive or toxic meetings, or the few minutes here and there lost scrolling when you only meant to check the time or reply to one text. It all adds up, and those leaks bleed out more than any workout ever puts in.

You wouldn't pour water into a cracked glass. You wouldn't wire money to an account with fraud alerts blinking red. But people try to build performance on top of holes they refuse to plug.

Leaks show up in three ways:

- Attention drain—constant noise, digital distraction, emotional spirals
- People tax—relationships that pull more than they give
- System friction—sloppy environments, endless meetings, poor travel habits

The biggest leak I see isn't just one bad meeting or one draining person—it's the cumulative damage of the constant noise. Phones buzzing. Algorithms pulling you sideways. Endless expectations about what you should be doing. Noise eats your attention before you've even chosen where to spend it.

That's why people feel like they're chasing their own tails. Buying the next program. Trying the next hack. Never actually moving forward. They're overloaded and disconnected. They've let noise run their system.

Protecting your energy means quieting that noise. Not numbing out, not escaping, but creating space where your OS can actually breathe. Until you do, every deposit will leak away before you can use it.

Plugging leaks isn't glamorous. It feels defensive, but it's what allows your deposits to actually compound. It's not enough to build your energy—you have to protect and maintain it. It's the only way you can get stronger.

THE EXECUTIVE WHO COULDN'T STOP

Another client of mine, a senior executive at a tech company, seemed to have it all—the fancy title, the big salary, and the coveted corner office. But when I started working with him, the cracks showed immediately. His calendar was a nightmare—back-to-back meetings from 7 AM to 7 PM. No breaks. No buffer, just a constant output. He'd walk from one high-stakes conversation straight into another, carrying all that tension forward.

By the time he got home, he had nothing left. He'd snap at his wife over small things and couldn't focus on his kids. Instead, he collapsed on the couch, scrolling on his phone until midnight. Then, he woke up exhausted and repeated the harmful cycle all over again.

He thought the problem was time management, and all he needed was a better calendar system or a new productivity app. But the problem wasn't his calendar. It was his energy ledger. So, we ran an audit. We tracked every meeting, every email check, every context switch, and mapped where he was building energy and where he was leaking it.

The results were brutal. He had almost no deposits—just constant withdrawals. Meetings with no agendas that ran long. Emails at all hours because notifications were always on. Lunch at his desk, scrolling news. Evenings spent trying to relax by staying plugged in.

He was never off. Never recovering. Just bleeding energy in a thousand small cuts.

So, we started plugging leaks. We limited him to two inbox windows per day instead of constant checking. Airplane mode during deep work blocks. A hard stop at 6 PM three days a week. Twenty-minute walks after lunch instead of doomscrolling. We protected his high-energy windows for the work that actually moved the needle.

Within two weeks, the shift was visible. Meetings that used to spiral into endless confusion now ended with crisp decisions. His team stopped walking on eggshells. At home, his wife said he seemed present for the first time in months. His kids noticed too.

The relief on his face when it clicked—that he didn't have to keep grinding every minute—was the same relief I'd seen in Aryna. And it was the same relief I had felt in the dojo all those years ago. Protecting your energy is learning how to manage your leaks so you can focus on doing what actually matters.

PEOPLE

Some conversations leave you heavier. Some meetings pull energy without ever pushing results. Throughout your week, pay attention to your energy during conversations. List the three conversations in your week that consistently drain you. Move them into low-stakes windows or set time caps. Protect your high-energy slots for work that matters.

DIGITAL

Phones and inboxes are designed to leak your attention—every swipe is a withdrawal. Give yourself two inbox windows per day. Block notifications during your focused work blocks.

MEETINGS

Meetings are often just organized leaks. No agenda means no meeting. Default to 25- or 50-minute slots. Guard the extra five or 10 minutes as time to reset before your next block.

TRAVEL

Jet lag, poor fuel, and rushed schedules can empty your account before you even land at your destination. Hydrate aggressively. Walk the terminal. On arrival, eat a light snack, get some movement, and find some sunlight. One hard rule—no major decisions the day you land.

SPEND: DIRECTING ENERGY WITH PRECISION

Most people spend energy the way they spend money on vacation: impulsively. They become scattered, and their money is gone before they know it. They waste it in the wrong places. I've watched athletes burn entire reserves on warm-ups. By the time the match starts, they're flat. I've seen executives spend their sharpest hours clearing email instead of making decisions. Parents leak their last ounce of focus into arguments that don't matter, then collapse when their kids actually need them.

The difference between fighters and warriors is precision. A fighter throws everything they have at the battle in front of them. A warrior chooses when to strike and when to hold back. That discipline makes the same unit of energy last longer, hit harder, and carry you further. Winning means facing the thing you're avoiding.

For Aryna, it came down to a technical fear.

THE SERVE THAT NEARLY BROKE HER

It was 2022, and Aryna's serve had been breaking down for months—double faults at the worst times, her confidence draining with every toss that felt wrong. But she wouldn't address it. She wouldn't even talk about it. She was terrified that if we started deconstructing her serve—toss, grip, footwork—the whole thing would unravel. She thought it was better to just keep fighting through it and grit it out. That's what fighters do.

Except it kept getting worse.

We watched her double-fault her way through matches she should have won. Week after week, tournament after tournament. The same breakdown. Her opponents knew it. They'd sit back and wait for her to beat herself. The press talked about it. Fans talked about it. Everyone could see the problem except for the one person who refused to look at it.

Aryna kept showing up. Kept practicing. Kept embarrassing herself. Kept feeling absolutely humiliated. That was the fighter—she just kept getting up, kept getting up, kept getting up. Good for her. She was as tough as hell, but it was getting her nowhere. She was spiraling downward into a giant mess—this monster of a thing we'd have to deal with. And all it would take to change the course was for her to face that one fear.

Finally, I had had enough.

It was in San Jose, halfway through the year. She lost the same way she'd been losing—serve falling apart, frustration spilling out. Afterward, she was crying, furious, exhausted, and stuck. "We've done everything," she said. "There's nothing else left."

I looked at her. "No. We've done everything except the one thing that scares you most. Do you want to keep fighting, or do you want to win?"

She knew exactly what I meant. "Do you want to keep just battling and banging your head through it—showing up, doing the same thing over and over again? Yeah, you're fighting. You're showing up. Big deal. But you're not making any progress. Or do you want to actually win?"

She stared at me before I continued. "Because if we don't address this—if you don't stand up, turn around, open your eyes, and face that biggest fear you have—then we're all stopping right now. There's no point in just banging your head against the wall. You've proven you're tough. You can keep showing up. But that's not good enough at this level. It got you to a certain point, but we're way beyond that."

That's when we brought in a specialist. Someone who could break down the mechanics without the emotional weight we carried as her coaches. We rebuilt her serve from the ground up. Toss. Grip. Footwork. Timing. All the things she'd been avoiding because facing them felt more dangerous than ignoring them.

It was brutal. She had to get worse before she got better. Had to trust the process when every instinct told her to go back to what felt familiar. Had to spend energy on the thing that terrified her instead of just grinding through matches, hoping it would fix itself.

But that's what precision looks like. Not just spreading energy everywhere but directing it to the root of the problem. Within weeks, her serve wasn't just fixed, it was better than it had ever been. The confidence came back. The rhythm returned. And more importantly, she learned that avoiding the hard thing costs more energy than facing it ever could.

That's the danger of unfocused spending. You can pour out massive energy and still lose if you aren't aiming it at the fears that are holding you back. Warriors direct energy into the hardest places because that's what creates transformation.

THE FLIGHT PLAN: TAKEOFF, CRUISE, DESCENT

It's helpful to think about energy like a flight plan. For an airplane, there are key moments along the journey that have different energy requirements. Namely, the takeoff, cruising, and then the descent. You should manage your energy following the same rhythm.

- Takeoff (prime): Short, sharp bursts of full intensity; 30–60 minutes of max focus with no distractions.
- Cruise (sustain): Steady output at an efficient rhythm; work 60–90 minutes, then a quick reset.
- Descent (recover): Deliberate downshift; take 20–30 minutes to close loops, review, and get set for tomorrow.

The problem is that too many people live in permanent takeoff mode—burning max thrust all the time until the engine flames out. Sustainable performance comes from cycling.

How to run it this week:

1. Pick one mission that deserves a takeoff block.
2. Block two cruise windows to execute steady work.
3. Schedule one descent ritual at the end of the day.

You don't need to master this all at once. Start with one clean takeoff block tomorrow. Experience the difference between full thrust and scattered output. To give this a little more context, my experience at the dojo gave me three principles that map directly onto the flight plan.

Zanshin is the awareness that extends before, during, and after the fight. Protecting and directing your energy works the same way. Takeoff isn't just about the sprint. It's about how you prepare before and how you reset after.

Mushin is no mind, the ability to move without hesitation once you've made a choice. That's cruise mode. Steady rhythm, free from overthinking.

Tomaranu kokoro, the indomitable spirit, is what carries you through descent when you'd rather quit.

These are reminders that energy isn't just physical fuel. It's awareness, rhythm, and spirit. Run your flight plan with those principles in mind. Awareness, rhythm, and spirit are what keep the cycle intact when pressure mounts.

WORKING WITH YOUR NATURAL RHYTHMS

Part of managing your energy is understanding your rhythms. When you peak. When you lag. What type of work fits which window.

At the broadest level, your energy follows a circadian rhythm—the daily cycle most people associate with sleep and wakefulness, light and dark. But it affects far more than when you go to bed. It influences when you're naturally alert, when effort feels clean, and when recovery actually works.[1]

Inside that larger daily rhythm are shorter cycles known as ultradian rhythms. These are the natural rises and falls in focus, intensity, and clarity that repeat throughout the day.[2] For most people, they run in waves of roughly 90 to 120 minutes. You feel them as stretches where you're sharp and engaged, followed by periods where attention drifts and everything takes more effort than it should.

Everyone recognizes this, even if they don't have language for it. The late-morning window where things click. The post-lunch dip where energy drops and focus fades. The second wind later in the day. These aren't motivation problems. They're rhythm shifts.

You can fight these cycles. People do it all the time—with caffeine, stimulants, adrenaline, or sheer grit. And in the short term, it works. But every time you override rhythm, you create stress. Over time, that stress accumulates. It shows up as mental fog, emotional reactivity, disrupted sleep, and a body that never quite recovers. That's how burnout happens. It's not all at once, but slowly, by ignoring signals you keep pushing past.

High performers take a different approach. They learn their rhythms and work with them. They schedule high-intensity, high-stakes work during natural peaks. They ride momentum during periods of clarity. And they deliberately downshift before fatigue turns into friction.

These rhythms aren't identical for everyone. The timing, height, and duration of your peaks and dips vary based on how you're built, the environment you're in, your health, and how aware you've become of your own signals. Some people are sharper early. Others come alive later. The most important thing is that you learn your waves. The more in tune you become with them, the smoother they run, and the more control you gain over your energy, your performance, and your overall well-being.

If you have control of your schedule, you schedule the right things at the right times. If you don't have control, you can learn how to manufacture the state you need for what's coming. You see this most clearly in elite performers like Formula 1 drivers, who spend their lives crossing time zones and living out of rhythm—where everyone faces the same disruption, and the edge goes to those who can adapt their energy fastest.

In the end, it's not about perfect timing or perfect conditions. It's about knowing your rhythms well enough to adjust on the fly and still show up as yourself when it counts.

WHEN YOU KNOW BETTER AND DO IT ANYWAY

If you can avoid it, you don't walk into a presentation during the window where you know you're flat. You don't schedule the hard conversation right after lunch when your body's in rest-and-digest mode. You learn your patterns, and you work with them—not against them.

I preach this.

I coach this.

I screw it up occasionally.

Case in point: I recently had an interview with ESPN, and it was garbage. They told me ahead of time what they wanted to talk about—the book, my work, the usual. So I started preparing. I listened to the audiobook. I reviewed my notes. I thought about how I'd answer different questions. I wanted to be ready.

But by the time I walked into that interview, I had so many thoughts swirling—bullet points, key messages, things I was "supposed to say"—that I wasn't present anymore. I was running through a mental checklist instead of being in the moment with the interviewer.

And then she asked me questions that I hadn't prepared for. I was scanning my prepared list instead of just listening and responding. So in response, I gave vague, general answers when she was looking for something specific. I could feel it happening, and I couldn't stop it.

The thing is—I absolutely knew better. I knew, while I was doing all that prep, that it was throwing me off. My gut was telling me: *Stop. You don't perform better this way. You perform better when you're clear on your values, present in the moment, and trusting yourself.* But I ignored it. I got caught up in what I thought I was supposed to do instead of what I know actually works for me.

Afterward, I ran the three big questions.

What worked? I showed up. I was professional. Maybe it was garbage (based on what I knew I could deliver), but it wasn't a disaster.

What needs work? I didn't listen to my gut. I overprepared in a way that pulled me out of presence. My attention was too broad—I had my mind on too many things and didn't narrow my focus to what the moment actually needed.

What's the plan? Next time, get clear on my intention—not my script. Trust that I know this material because I've lived it. Show up ready to be in the room, not ready to perform a rehearsed version of myself.

That same week, I had two more live national television appearances. I recorded two podcast interviews. I did a long-form interview with the *Australian Financial Review* magazine. And every single one of them went fan-freaking-tastic.

They flowed. I was articulate. I got the message across. I connected with the interviewers. I was present. People reached out afterward telling me how clear it was, how much it resonated, how powerful it felt.

The difference between the interviews wasn't more preparation. It was *better* preparation.

That ESPN interview was a slap-in-the-face reminder. I didn't listen to my gut and prepare the way I know works for me. I crossed the line from clarity into control, from intention into rehearsal. I overthought it. And I paid for it with a performance that didn't reflect who I am or how I actually work at my best.

That's why the audit matters.

It doesn't keep you from messing up, but it shortens the gap between the mistake and the correction. It reminds you that this work isn't about being perfect. It's about paying attention. About knowing the right amount of focus, intensity, and arousal you need for this moment—and trusting yourself enough to stay there.

We're human, and sometimes we will miss. But we can learn how to catch it and reset. And when we do, the results take care of themselves.

THE SEVEN-DAY ENERGY AUDIT

Most people have no idea where their energy actually goes. This audit will show you in seven days.

DAYS 1–2: TRACK EVERYTHING

Carry a notebook or use your phone. Every time you feel an energy shift—up or down—write it down. What were you doing? Who were you with? What had you just eaten, read, or experienced?

Don't judge it. Don't fix it yet. Just observe.

DAY 3: IDENTIFY THE TOP-THREE LEAKS

Look at your notes. Circle the patterns. Which three things consistently drain you? Maybe it's certain people. Certain times of day. Certain types of work. Certain digital habits.

Pick one leak you'll protect against starting tomorrow.

DAYS 4–5: ADD TAKEOFF BLOCKS

Schedule one 30-minute takeoff block each day. Pick your highest-leverage work. Turn off notifications. Close the door. Run the reset loop before you start: Roll your shoulders back, open your chest, breathe twice, set your posture, and aim at one clear task.

Notice how different this feels from scattered work.

DAY 6: PLAN YOUR DESCENT

At the end of the day, instead of just stopping, create a shutdown ritual. Close open loops. Write down tomorrow's first move. Spend five minutes reviewing what worked well, what needs work, and what the plan is.

This will clear your mental cache so you're not carrying today's weight into tomorrow.

DAY 7: REVIEW THE LEDGER

At the end of the week, look at your full audit. Did you build more than you burned? Where did rhythm hold? Where did it break?

This is how you see your operating system. Most people never do this. They just keep running the same buggy code, wondering why their performance crashes at the worst times.

The audit isn't meant to be a one-time thing. It's a practice. Weekly at first, and then monthly once you've got the basics dialed in. The goal is simple: Learn to see your energy clearly so you can manage it deliberately.

RESOLUTION: ENERGY ISN'T A MOOD

Energy is the foundation of the Performance OS. It's a system you build, protect, and use. Ignore it, and you run into an overdraft: snapping at your kids, fogging out in meetings, burning out on the court. Respect it, and everything else opens up: emotion steadies, environment sharpens, decisions become clearer, trust grows.

For the next seven days, run your first energy audit.

- Track deposits, leaks, and spending.
- Add one takeoff block where you put your full energy into the thing that matters most.
- Protect one boundary. No excuses.
- At the end of the week, review your ledger. Did you build more than you burned? Did rhythm hold or break?

This is how you install your Pressure Code: with habits, not hacks; with infrastructure, not inspiration. Never forget that energy is currency. Manage it as if your freedom depends on it—because it does.

When you're able to manage your energy, you'll do more than just keep yourself steady. You'll build trust. People will know whether you'll show up calm or chaotic, present or scattered. Through loyalty to your own system comes trust from others. With that trust comes freedom—the freedom to take risks, to lead, to create. And to maintain that freedom, you have to remain loyal to the habits that built it in the first place.

Energy isn't just about you. It's about credibility. If people can count on your energy, they can count on you. That's why energy is the first E. Without it, emotions and environment collapse. With it, the rest of the OS has the fuel it needs to run effectively.

Chapter Four

EMOTIONS: SIGNALS, NOT ENEMIES

At the Australian Open, Aryna Sabalenka looked like two different athletes. One minute, she was crushing serves and blasting forehands that nobody could touch. The next minute, her shoulders sagged, her face collapsed, and she was criticizing herself under her breath. When the errors piled up, the racket came down hard. The stadium didn't need the scoreboard—they could read the match on her body.

Everyone watching thought the same thing: She's too emotional.

That's the common story we tell ourselves too. We label our emotions as weakness. We try to suppress them, hide them, or blow them off. But emotions aren't the enemy. They're signals. Aryna wasn't losing because she had emotions. She was losing because she didn't know how to use them. Her body was broadcasting information—shoulders, breath, tone, posture—but instead of receiving the message and responding, she let the signal run her.

The same thing that happens on the court takes place at the office, in the classroom, and at home. A leader gets frustrated and leaks it into the room. A teacher lets their own overwhelm spill into the way they correct a student. A coach loses composure on the sideline, and the players mirror it. A parent drags the day's stress into dinner and snaps at their kid. The emotion itself isn't the problem. The problem is letting the signal drive instead of reading it for what it is.

EMOTIONS ARE DATA

There's a lot of baggage when it comes to emotions. We've been taught to treat them like enemies—to be suppressed, hidden, or blown off. From the time we're kids, we hear those damaging messages: Stop crying. Shake it off. Don't let them see you sweat. By the time we're adults, the playbook hasn't changed. Leaders are told to keep a stiff upper lip, athletes are told to tough it out, and parents are told not to show weakness in front of their kids. The message is clear: Emotions make you fragile.

But that's backward. Emotions come with being human. When you suppress them, they don't disappear; they get louder until they hijack you. When you explode, you're letting the raw signal run the system. Both cost energy, and both erode trust. That's why Aryna kept unraveling. Her body was broadcasting signals, but without a system to read the signal, she defaulted to what most people do: reacting. And when you react, the emotion drives.

Emotions aren't directives. They're data—information about your state, your environment, your needs. Anger might tell you a boundary has been crossed. Fear might tell you that you're unprepared. Sadness might tell you something needs to be grieved. Ignore the data, and you miss the message.

Once Aryna understood this, everything shifted. Her job wasn't to erase her emotions. It was to read them, then reset. Shoulders dropping meant her system was tightening. Breath shortening meant fear was creeping in. A flash of anger meant her focus had drifted from the plan to the problem. Instead of reacting, she started responding.

That's the skill: to notice the signal, pause, and choose. But most people never get that far. They live at the mercy of whatever emotion shows up—amped up when adrenaline spikes, flattened by anxiety attacks, reckless when anger flares. Warriors learn to see emotions as dashboards, not drivers. They scan, they interpret, and then they act.

SIGNALS IN THE STREETS

When I ended up on the streets as a child, accurately reading emotions became essential to my survival. Violence could come out of nowhere. I learned to read a room the way other kids read textbooks. A shift in laughter. Shoulders squaring. A sudden silence in the wrong place. Ignore these signals, and you'd pay the price.

When I finally found the dojo, I realized the same skill showed up on the mats. *Zanshin* is the awareness before, during, and after the fight. It meant paying attention not only to your opponent, but to yourself. Was your breath steady? Was your jaw locked? Was your mind already racing ahead or stuck replaying the last mistake?

That's what Aryna was missing. Her body was screaming out signals, but she wasn't trained to notice them. In the dojo, I learned that micro-signals dictate the fight long before the punch lands. On the court, it's the same. A warrior learns to see the signals, reset, and re-engage.

CONTAGION IN THE ROOM

There's another layer to signals most people don't think about: They spread. Your emotions leak out and affect those around you. Science shows your body literally releases chemical signals about your emotional state. Fear, stress, and even joy get transmitted through sweat, and the people around you absorb it without even knowing why. Research on chemosignals proves it: Smell alone can make another person's heart rate rise, breathing shift, or muscles tense. Your team reads more than body language. They can literally smell your emotional state.[3]

That's why a tense locker room can rattle an entire team before a match. It's why one anxious executive can walk into a meeting and shift the mood without saying a word. And it's why your state as a parent, coach, or leader matters more than what you tell people. They feel you before they hear you.

The lesson is simple: When you manage your emotions, you're shaping the emotional climate for everyone in the room.

RESETTING THE SIGNAL

The first step in turning your emotions to your advantage is noticing the signal. The second is resetting the signal, and that's where most people fail. They either react instantly or try to suppress it, and both burn energy. Resetting is about creating space to respond with intention.

In martial arts, that space comes in the pause between moves. On the court, it comes between points. In everyday life, it comes between the moment you feel the surge of emotion and the words or actions that follow. Here's the loop I teach world-class athletes (and everyone else):

1. Drop: Release tension with a long exhale. Roll back your shoulders and keep your chest open, jaw loose, and hands unclenched.

2. Breathe: In through the nose, out longer through the mouth. Two cycles are enough to change your state.
3. Set: Restack your posture—feet grounded, eyes up, face calm.
4. Aim: Choose one clear next action. Not three, not five—one.

Aryna used this loop in matches, but I've watched leaders use it before walking into boardrooms, or parents use it before walking into their kitchen at the end of a long day. It doesn't erase the emotion but instead redirects it. Resetting the signal gives you the chance to read the data before deciding how to use it.

THE EMOTIONAL RESET

Remember, emotions aren't the enemy. They're signals—messengers from the body trying to tell you what's off. The problem is that we can sometimes get stuck in our emotions. Every elite performer eventually learns the same lesson: Recovery between moments matters more than control inside them. The best performers are fluent in their emotions. They know how to let a wave hit, process it, and move on before it hijacks the next play, meeting, or conversation. When I coach athletes through this, we don't talk about mindset first. We start with the body. The fastest way to reset emotions is to reset physiology.

THE RESET LOOP

When the system starts to spin, it's time to run a simple sequence: Roll, breathe, set, aim. Roll your shoulders back. Open your chest. Unclench your jaw. Let the air out completely. Most people breathe out halfway and call it done, which keeps tension trapped. Breathe in for four seconds through your nose and out for six through your mouth—three rounds, slow and controlled. Set your posture: tall spine, soft knees, open chest. The body teaches the brain what readiness feels like. Then, aim—ask yourself, "What does this moment require?" not, "What do I feel like doing?"

That question turns impulse into intention. The whole loop takes less than a minute, but it resets your chemistry, posture, and focus in one move.

THRESHOLD RITUALS

We carry emotional residue from one environment into the next. Most people don't realize it until their family gets the version of them meant for the boardroom, or their teammates get the emotional leftovers from home.

Before you cross a doorway, pause. Exhale once through your mouth. Roll your shoulders back. Inhale calm through your nose and exhale whatever you're done with. Mentally say, *Leave that behind*, and enter the next moment cleanly. That single breath between environments can change an entire evening. It's how you teach your system to reset on command.

THE 90-SECOND WINDOW

Neuroscience has shown that the chemical surge of any raw emotion—anger, fear, frustration—lasts about 90 seconds.[4] After that, the emotion only lives on if the story keeps feeding it.

So, when the spike hits, don't react. Breathe. Count out a minute and a half before you move, speak, or hit send. By the end, the charge fades enough for logic to return. Remember, you're not trying to repress the emotion; you're simply waiting for the chemistry to pass so you can respond instead of retaliating.

AFTER THE REACTION

When you slip—and you will—use this information as feedback, not a sign of failure. Ask yourself a few quick questions:

- What was I actually feeling?
- What triggered it?
- What did my body do in that moment?
- What did I do with that energy?

Each answer shows where the signal broke and where awareness dropped.

FAST RESETS THAT WORK ANYWHERE

Before a big meeting or match, take three strong inhales through your nose, three long exhales through your mouth, and square your stance.

After a mistake, run two slow sighs—the double inhale, long exhale—and roll your shoulders back, opening your chest.

In conflict, soften your eyes, slow your exhale, and listen fully before speaking.

At the end of the day, take a short walk in silence and breathe longer than you think you need to.

No matter the situation, slowing down and resetting allows you to regain control and process your emotions with intention.

LEADING THROUGH EMOTION

When you hold composure, everyone watching you borrows it. On teams, emotion is a chemical contagion—all your nervous systems are in sync. As a result, calm leadership often means metabolizing emotion faster than the people around you.

Start a meeting with one collective breath. Pause after conflict instead of filling the silence. Reflect out loud when emotion shaped a decision. Those moments teach more than speeches ever could.

SOMETIMES YOU SCREAM

I've talked a lot about resetting inward. Roll the shoulders back. Open your chest. Slow the breath. Find your posture. Settle the noise.

But sometimes you need to go the other direction. Sometimes you need to express *outward.*

There's a New Zealand rugby team, the All Blacks. They're widely regarded as the most successful team in the history of international sport, not just because of how often they win, but because of the culture they've built to sustain that level of performance over decades.

One of their longtime captains, Richie McCaw, had a simple ritual. Before critical moments, he'd repeatedly stomp his foot on the ground as hard as he could. It was his way of reminding himself that he was strong, grounded, and connected to the earth. It was his trigger for readiness.

That wasn't unique to him. Another captain would look up toward the top of the stadium when he felt himself drifting, using perspective to pull himself back into the moment. Some players used breathing. Others clasped their hands. One young star, rising fast and surrounded by hype, had a coach who would quietly tap his shoe against the player's cleat. No words, just a simple reminder: *Stay grounded.*

The All Blacks understand that pressure doesn't disappear at the highest level—it multiplies. Expectations rise. Attention grows. Ego creeps in. Their edge isn't avoiding emotion, but knowing how to regulate it and stay clear under pressure.

People ask me about Aryna all the time. They see her yell

mid-match. They see her smash a racket. And they wonder: *How is that okay? Isn't she supposed to be composed?*

What they don't understand is sometimes there's so much built up inside—tension, pressure, emotion—that the only way back to center is through release. Not suppression. Release.

During a match, Aryna will suddenly let out this yell. Out of nowhere. And then—boom—she's back. Locked in. The yell clears the static.

Now, I'm not suggesting you slam your fist on the table in a board meeting and say, "Okay, I'm ready. What were we discussing?" There's a time and place for outwardly resetting. But understand that you have options.

Some people need to go inward to find their center. Others need to express outward to get there. And sometimes, the same person needs different things on different days.

The goal isn't one technique. The goal is awareness—knowing what you need in this moment to perform your best. And having the courage to do it.

THE FOUR STATES OF PERFORMANCE

Managing your emotions is about dialing in to the right state for the moment. I think of it like a dashboard with four dials I can adjust. Turn one up, ease one down. Constant calibration puts you in the right state to perform your best.

The four dials are arousal, attention, focus, and intensity.

- Arousal is your baseline charge. Too low, and you're flat. Too high, and you're jittery.
- Attention is broad awareness. Where is your energy scattering or spreading?

- Focus is narrowing that attention to one target. Zoom too wide, and you get overwhelmed. Zoom too tight, and you miss what matters.
- Intensity is the force you bring, how much power you pour into the moment.

The art is knowing which one to turn up or down. Before you enter the arena of your choice, scan the dashboard. Too much intensity? Dial it down. Attention scattered? Narrow it.

CALIBRATING THE FOUR DIALS

When I'm with an athlete or executive before a big moment, we always start here. No theory, no mindset talk, just a quick scan to see how the system's running. It takes less than two minutes, but it tells you everything.

AROUSAL—YOUR INTERNAL RPM

You can feel this one before you name it. It's the body's engine speed, or revolutions per minute (RPM). Too low and you're heavy, slow to engage, almost disconnected. Too high and you're jittery, short of breath, reactionary.

Ask yourself: Where's my body's RPM right now—under-revving or redlining?

When you're flat, wake the system up with fast nasal breaths—two seconds in, two out—for about a minute. Roll the shoulders. Move. The goal is a gentle lift, not adrenaline.

When you're overamped, slow everything down. Two slow inhales through the nose, one long exhale through the mouth. Roll the shoulders back and open your chest. Let the air leave completely. You'll feel your pulse settle.

ATTENTION—WHERE THE LIGHT IS POINTING

Attention is the direction and width of your mental spotlight. Some days, it's too wide—you're taking in too much, missing what matters. Other times, it's too narrow—you're tunneled in, losing context.

Ask: Am I scanning too wide or gripping too tight?

If you're scattered, pick one visual anchor. A face. A line on the court. A single object in the room. Stay with it until your vision steadies.

If you're overlocked, zoom out. Soften your gaze. Look to the edge of your field of vision. Take one long exhale and let the room widen again.

FOCUS—DEPTH OF ENGAGEMENT

Focus is how long you can hold your attention where it matters. When it's shallow, your thoughts drift; when it's hyper, you forget to breathe.

If you're bouncing between tasks, anchor yourself for two minutes—steady posture, quiet breath, eyes on one fixed point. If you're overlocked, stand up, stretch, blink, and zoom out before re-engaging.

Optimal focus should feel effortless, not forced. It's what happens when attention and arousal are in sync.

INTENSITY—FORCE OF EXPRESSION

Intensity is the emotional volume of your performance. It's the throttle.

A low level of intensity feels detached, like you're just going through the motions. Overintensity feels like you're forcing power you don't have—gripping too tight, overtalking, overswinging.

When you're low, add drive: three sharp inhales through the nose, three slow exhales through the mouth. Stand tall, raise your posture, and feel your presence build.

When you're too high, slow your breath—six seconds in, six out—and ground your feet. Drop the need to prove and return to connection.

Cue yourself quietly: Deliver power, not panic.

RUNNING THE CALIBRATION LOOP

Before any key event—meeting, match, negotiation—take 90 seconds to check the system.

- Close your eyes.
- Name where each dial sits from one to ten.
    - Arousal too high? Slow the breath.
    - Attention scattered? Find a single focal point.
    - Focus drifting? Reanchor your posture and breath.
    - Intensity spiking? Exhale longer than you inhale.
- Then open your eyes, settle into a soft focus, and take one full exhale before you move.
- Do it again. Notice what has shifted.

The goal here is to recognize drift and steer back before you spin out. The more you track the dials, the faster you'll sense the moment they start to slip—and the quicker you'll bring them back into rhythm.

NAMING THE SIGNAL

There's one more move that helps strip emotions of their power: naming them. Research shows that when you put words to what you feel, the intensity drops. Your brain shifts from raw reaction to recognition.

On the streets, I didn't have research language for it, but I practiced it every day. Fear. Anger. Grief. I'd feel it rising and call it out, even just in my head. Naming it gave me enough distance to choose what came next instead of letting the feeling run me. That practice kept me alive more than once. Later, in the dojo, I learned the philosophy and science behind that practice—labeling an emotion lowers its intensity and gives you back a choice.

With me, Aryna learned the same principle. Instead of trying to bury her frustration, she started saying it: "I'm tight." "I'm angry." Once the emotion had a name, it stopped driving the bus. The moment she acknowledged it, she could run the reset loop and take control of the next point.

Telling yourself "I'm anxious" before a meeting is a far better strategy than pretending you're fine. Admitting "I'm drained" before you walk into dinner with your family is better than snapping and later pretending it didn't happen. Naming the emotion enables you to react with awareness.

CARRYOVER COSTS

It's not just athletes who get derailed by emotion. I've coached executives who walked out of one high-stakes meeting and carried all that tension straight into the next room—or worse, straight into their homes. They thought they were compartmentalizing, but their team felt the weight, and their families got the scraps.

The breakthrough came when they learned to treat emotion like data and run a reset ritual before crossing thresholds. Adding in 10 minutes of breathwork between back-to-back meetings and a walk around the block before walking through the front door were simple moves, but they cut the carryover. Because if you don't clear stress, it will infect every room you walk into. Managing your emotions will protect you and the people around you.

EMOTIONS ALIGNED

When energy runs the OS, emotions become the dashboard. Ignore them, and you crash. Overreact, and you oversteer. But read them, reset them, and name them—and emotions become fuel for clarity, rhythm, and trust.

That's the move from fighter to warrior. Fighters get hijacked by every reactive surge. Warriors read the signal, reset their state, and move forward on purpose. This is why emotions come second in the running of your Pressure Code. Energy gives you the currency, but emotions tell you where it's being spent. Align the two, and you stop living at the mercy of moods and start using them as momentum.

And once emotions steady, the next lever of influence becomes clear: the environment you create and the one you carry with you.

Chapter Five

ENVIRONMENT: THE HIDDEN LEVER

At Wimbledon, Aryna Sabalenka carried a grudge. She called it her "hate relationship" with the grass. Before a ball was even struck, her posture gave her away. The surface felt wrong, the press was heavy, and the crowd was tight. She walked onto the court already shrinking, feeling that Wimbledon was doing its best to beat her before the first serve.

That's the power of your environment. It's more than your surroundings; it's how you're shaped by them—something I understood long before I coached Aryna. In my youth, my environment was violence, drugs, and crime rates through the roof. It pressed down on everything. Most kids got swallowed up by it. I almost did too. What saved me were the rare environments that offered me something different—the library, where I could disappear into silence, and the dojo, where I learned to replace chaos with order. Those places didn't just shelter me; they showed me a different way to be.

Environments aren't neutral: They either elevate or erode you.

Aryna's grass courts. My streets. Your office, a court, the living room, your kitchen. You can pretend to ignore them, but you'll find out the hard way: *Your environment always wins.*

People love to preach willpower. Tough it out. Push harder. Rise above. But the research is clear: Willpower is fragile, but the environment is dominant. Psychologist Kurt Lewin put it bluntly: Behavior is a function of the person and their environment. Change the environment, and the behavior shifts—whether you intend it to or not.[5]

Cafeteria studies show that moving fruit to eye level changes eating habits more than a lecture on nutrition.[6] Cluttered spaces raise cortisol and scatter attention. Noisy offices undermine memory and problem-solving. Even the famous Marshmallow Test for self-control turned out not to be about grit. The researchers found that children from more stable or higher-trust environments were more likely to wait. This was not necessarily because of superior self-control, but because they could trust the adult's promise that the reward would actually come.[7]

That's why "just try harder" doesn't work. You can grind for a while, but the environment will always bend you back to the shape it predetermines. The choice is simple: Either you shape your environment, or it shapes you. There's no neutral ground.

SHAPE OR BE SHAPED

You don't just live in your environment—you carry it. Every setting you walk into either raises or lowers your ceiling. I tell clients all the time: Show me your environment and I'll show you your performance ceiling.

This is simply a matter of physics. Noise, clutter, toxic people, and endless notifications all pull your energy before you even begin.

On the flip side, when you step into a space that's ordered, quiet, and charged with trust, your system lifts. You think more sharply, move more freely, and perform better.

ENVIRONMENT IN ACTION

Aryna's story makes this principle obvious. At Wimbledon—the grass, the press, the energy in the stands—it all stacked against her. But the same player walked into the US Open with different cues, different rituals, and a different charge in the environment. The court felt like home. The energy lifted her instead of pressing her down. Same athlete. Two different environments. Two very different outcomes.

One executive I worked with couldn't figure out why his team was always scattered and reactive. His calendar was packed with back-to-back meetings, his office was cluttered, and his digital environment was nonstop notifications. His environment guaranteed he never had any focus. Once we stripped out the noise, built in resets, and set guardrails, the same leader looked completely different. His team didn't change. His environment did.

At one time, I used to run a gym. Not a boutique wellness spot with curated playlists and eucalyptus towels—a real gym. Concrete floors. Chalk in the air. The kind of place where the mirrors are cracked, and the sound system rattles when someone drops a deadlift.

That's where I met Ryan.

He wasn't a headline case. No sponsorships. No social following. Just a young man in his twenties with a nervous system at war with itself. He was born with severe scoliosis and neurological challenges, and his body had learned to brace for impact—even when none was coming. His gait was uneven, his posture collapsed, and his eyes darted to the ground like he was waiting to apologize for existing.

He came to us through a wellness program that paired disabled clients with fitness professionals. On paper, the goal was "light activity for improved quality of life." Translation: Keep him busy; don't expect change. From the moment he walked in, I could feel the weight of every good intention that had quietly crushed him. His family loved him. His caretakers adored him. But their love had become protection, and that protection had become permission to stay small, dependent, careful.

That's the danger of safety—it masquerades as kindness.

The first day, he arrived flanked by two helpers holding his arms as if the air itself was too risky. I smiled, thanked them, and said, "Let's see what he can do."

They hesitated. Hovered. You could feel the panic. The unspoken *What if he falls?*

And he did fall. Almost immediately.

But that's where the work began. I had him stand again, alone this time. Ten seconds on his own legs. Shaking. Eyes wide. Every muscle of his screaming to sit back down.

He looked at me, frustrated. "I can't."

I nodded. "Okay. Then we'll do it again."

He didn't know it yet, but that moment was the start of his rebuild. Yes, muscle, but mostly belief. And belief is built through exposure, not encouragement.

If you're always caught, you never learn balance.

If you're always protected, you never build power.

If you're always rescued, you never have the opportunity to rise.

So, we built slowly. No miracle hacks. No motivational speeches. Just consistent micro-adjustments—posture, breath, awareness. Some days we boxed, if you can call it that. I'd hold pads while he threw slow, crooked jabs. He missed half the time, but each swing rewired his trust in himself.

Six months later, he was walking across the turf without help.

A year in, he could spar lightly. Two years in, he was training alone. Every step was an act of rebellion against the environment that had taught him to stay still. The hardest transformation didn't take place in Ryan's muscles—it was in the people who loved him most. Every session, I'd watch him leave the gym and get swallowed by a crowd of caretakers—arms out, voices soft, eager to steady him before he even stumbled. Every act of help was another line of code reinforcing the same story: You can't.

One afternoon, after he'd taken 10 clean, unassisted steps, his mother rushed forward with a towel and said, "Careful, honey, don't overdo it."

He looked down again. The victory drained out of him before the sweat could dry. That's when I pulled her aside and asked, "Do you want him safe or do you want him strong?"

She froze. No one had ever asked her that. Safety had become her religion. But safety only builds dependence. So, I started teaching the whole family the same lesson I was teaching Ryan: Support isn't doing it for him; it's standing close enough for him to do it himself.

We built boundaries and then rituals. When he walked through the door, nobody touched him unless he asked. No one carried his bag. No one finished his sentences. They hated it at first. It felt cold, even cruel. But slowly, they began to see what I saw: Every unnecessary hand was stealing a little more of his independence.

Of course, they meant well. They tried hard. But they had held him down. That's the paradox of care—it can smother the very life it's trying to protect. And if you've ever led a team, raised a kid, or coached someone through growth, you've likely experienced the same thing. The instinct to shield is strong, but the best coaches exercise the discipline to step back.

One day, Ryan walked in angry. He'd been scolded for training too long and "pushing too far."

He dropped his gym bag and said, "They keep telling me I'm

doing too much. But they don't know what it feels like to finally move."

He looked at me, waiting for sympathy. Instead, I said, "Maybe they're right."

His face fell. Then I added, "Maybe you are pushing too far—but for the first time, it's you doing the pushing."

He laughed—just once, sharp and loud—and that laugh broke something open.

I continued, "Every system fights the change that threatens it. Even your own. That's why this feels like resistance. But what you're really feeling is growth."

From that day forward, we stopped talking about exercise and started talking about environmental regulation. His living space, his routines, even his playlists—all were restructured to reinforce his autonomy. He learned to design micro-environments inside his world, from the way his room was laid out and the order of his morning to the people around him, understanding each person's intentions, their influence on him, and when their presence supported his growth versus when it held him back. The placement of reminders that whispered the new narrative—stand tall, breathe, walk again.

Change the environment.

Change the behavior.

Change the belief.

Change the life.

By the time he could walk across the gym unaided, his body had caught up to a truth his mind finally believed: He was not broken, just poorly trained.

The last day he worked with me, he came in alone. No helpers. No family. Just a duffel bag, a crooked smile, and a gait that still wobbled but didn't apologize for it. He told me he was moving to another city to live on his own. I asked if he was scared.

"A little."

"Good," I replied. "That means you're alive."

He nodded, then said something I'll never forget: "You were the first person who stopped helping me."

That line hit harder than any punch I've ever taken. Because that's what real coaching is: refusing to make someone smaller so they'll feel safe near you. He left that day taller—not just physically but spiritually, like gravity had finally lost its grip.

Performance begins whenever a human decides to change the environment that defines them. Ryan taught me that comfort is the enemy of capability. Even love left unexamined can become a leash. That growth isn't about what you add. It's about what you remove: interference, indulgence, unnecessary hands.

If you're surrounded by people who constantly make things easier, be careful. Ease is a slow anesthetic that numbs you into smallness. The right environment doesn't coddle you; it calls you higher. It doesn't protect your weakness; it exposes your strength. That's what loyalty looks like at its highest form—one that demands your evolution.

Ryan's story reflects a universal lesson: Your environment is an essential component of your Pressure Code. The people, spaces, and signals around you are constantly training your nervous system. Every conversation, every relationship, every community you stay connected to is shaping your internal state. The science backs it. Across cultures, the single strongest predictor of happiness, health, and even how long you live isn't wealth or discipline—it's connection.[8]

Strong relationships don't just protect your heart; they protect your drive. They keep purpose alive when discipline runs out. The opposite is also true. The wrong people, the wrong rooms, will drain your nervous system faster than any bad habit. The people around you determine your rhythm, your recovery, and your reach.

BUILDING YOUR ENVIRONMENT

If the environment always wins, the only power we have is to shape it. Here are the levers I use to make sure the environment is working for us, not against us.

AUDIT THE ENVIRONMENT

Every space speaks. Air, light, sound, and faces all tell your body how to be. Top performers listen, ignoring the noise and holding on to their energy.

Start where you stand.

Your physical environment trains your nervous system long before you act. Clutter keeps attention on alert. Noise keeps tension half-loaded. When a room breathes, you breathe with it. Order is clarity made visible.

Your digital environment hums around you like static. Each alert, each open tab, calls for a fraction of your focus. What you check first each morning teaches your brain what to chase.

Your relational environment carries its own weather. Spend enough time in storms, and you start dressing for rain. Choose the people who sharpen your awareness, who steady your breathing.

And then there's your internal environment—the one that follows you everywhere. The voice in your head, the set of your shoulders, the breath that shortens when stress hits. If that world stays chaotic, every other fix is temporary. Awareness is the first repair.

Once you can see the pattern, begin the edit. Shift one thing in each domain. That might mean clearing a surface or silencing a device. Whatever the action, it requires the courage to be honest with yourself first. Then, extend that same level of honesty to others. There will be times when you need to call people out in your environment to help them get back on track. Sometimes that means a subtle knowing look or nudge, and sometimes that means a deep intervention.

That's the 3–3–3 Rule: Try making three small edits each week for three weeks. This creates a simple rhythm that produces a steady return. And remember, awareness itself creates pressure. When you start noticing what supports you and what drains you, things begin to shift.

I once had a young trainer who felt trapped in a toxic gym culture. He couldn't leave—he needed the paycheck. So, he started doing daily audits. After every client session or team interaction, he'd do a quick gut check: What worked? What felt off? What gave me energy? What took it?

No judgment or drama. Just awareness.

At first, nothing around him changed. But slowly, because he was tracking the signals, he began to see patterns. He noticed which people steadied him, which hours drained him, which conversations pulled him out of alignment. That awareness became leverage.

Within a year, he'd pivoted from personal training to running workshops for other young coaches. He built a business teaching the very mindset that once held him back. And that's what awareness does—it puts quiet pressure on the system until something gives.

If you can't change where you are right now, start by seeing it clearly. That clarity alone begins the shift. Start with a simple scan physically, digitally, and relationally.

- Physical: Is your space clean, ordered, and charged with purpose—or cluttered and draining?
- Digital: Do notifications and pings own you, or do you control them?
- Relational: Are the people around you fueling you or bleeding you?

An audit is about clarity. Once you see the leaks, you can start plugging them.

NOISE VERSUS FOUNDATION

Noise is everything that scatters your attention—clutter, excess inputs, toxic people. Foundations are the cues that ground you—rituals, routines, order. Strip the noise first. Then, stack your foundations so the environment resets you automatically.

CUES AND TRIGGERS

Environments run on signals. Light, sound, scent, posture—they all program behavior. Use them on purpose. A bright light in the morning cues alertness. Music or scent can anchor you in focus. Even posture—how you sit down at your desk—can trigger the shift into work mode.

PEOPLE AND PROXIMITY

Meaningful work is more than achievement; it's about connection. You can have every ergonomic setup and still be starving inside if the people around you are draining you instead of feeding you. The most powerful environments I've seen are the ones built on relationships. The quality of your relationships determines how long you last, how deeply you grow, and how much joy you allow yourself to feel.

When you think about managing your environment, think about your circle.

Who helps you reset?

Who brings energy instead of noise?

Who challenges you without draining you?

Performance is sustained by belonging. And in the end, just like your code, you rise or fall to the level of those who surround you.

So, put yourself in environments where discipline, honesty, and excellence are the standard. Then protect yourself from the opposite.

I saw it play out with Aryna. Early in her career, the people closest to her—handlers, teammates, and media staff—were nervous. They carried their anxiety into her space, which then bled into her game. So, I made it my job to step between her and that noise. Sometimes literally. If someone's energy was off, I knew they didn't belong in the room. I told them to leave. Not because I wanted to be the guy in control, but because I understood that her environment mattered more than other people's comfort.

That's how vital proximity is. One shaky voice can unravel a competitor. One calm, trusted presence can reset them. Your environment isn't just walls and screens—it's people. Choose them carefully and don't be afraid to guard that space with teeth.

Here are a few examples from my life.

The dojo didn't just teach me how to fight. It gave me a family. Jeremy, another student I trained alongside every day, and Tom, an older instructor and mentor, were like brothers. The Patawaran family—mom, dad, and three daughters—became the people who held me up when I had no one. I met them through the kids' classes I was helping with; their daughters were students, and over time their whole family became part of my life. They called me their adopted son, and eventually, that's what I became.

I started tagging along to soccer games and family barbecues. Before long, I was sleeping on their couch most weekends. Half the time, I didn't even talk much—I'd just sit there while everyone else went about their lives. That house was alive, and safe—you could feel the trust in the air. I knew I needed to be around it, so I kept showing up. Every weekend, every game, every dinner.

Eventually, they just folded me in. I became the big brother, the extra son. That environment didn't just shape my body. It rebuilt my sense of what could be: the right people, the right energy, the right rhythm. It taught me that sometimes the fastest way to heal is through belonging.

I experienced this at another critical time in my life. I was 20, working at a Sleep Number store with two women—Betty and Charlene—who could not have been more different from me. Betty was loud, funny, Southern, and always telling stories. Charlene was quiet. Centered. The kind of presence that made you notice your own breathing.

At the time, I was still jumpy—always keeping a certain distance from people without realizing it. Charlene would laugh about it and test me, stepping closer until I'd lean away, then backing off just to see if I'd lean forward. She was teaching me awareness without ever saying a word. But what she really taught me was how to be vulnerable. Not weak—*vulnerable.*

I'd have these violent dreams that would play on repeat—dark, chaotic, full of fear. She'd listen to me talk about them while we worked but never tried to fix me. She just listened and said, "You have the power to guide what happens next."

Her way of helping wasn't through answers. It was through presence. Sometimes she'd just stand in front of me, hands open, calm and unshakable. It was like she was saying, *You're safe here. You can stop bracing.* That was the first time I started to believe that strength and openness weren't opposites. They were the same thing expressed at different frequencies.

Years later, I watched the same pattern unfold with Aryna. The same fight between control and surrender. The same need to open the smallest crack of vulnerability so real power could come through.

Charlene used to tell me, "It's not about this or that—it is what it is." She even had a small tattoo of a spiral, a reminder that life doesn't move in straight lines, that you revisit lessons at higher levels. That spiral shows up everywhere in my work now—how athletes evolve, how emotions recycle, how energy flows.

I didn't understand it then, but she was the first person who taught me what presence really looks like. No performance, no agenda. Just pure awareness. That's the state every great leader, every champion, every parent I've coached is trying to reach.

Meeting Charlene was one of those moments you don't see coming. But looking back, I know it was meant to be. She sparked a key turning point in my life and helped me further understand myself in ways the dojo couldn't teach. The mats gave me discipline, but Charlene gave me permission to be human.

That lesson—things are just the way they are—became foundational to how I coach. When Aryna spirals, when executives panic, when someone's system breaks under pressure, I don't freak out. I just see it clearly. Things are the way they are. Now, let's figure out what to do about it. That insight came from having the right person in my life at the right time. The power of the people around you, for good and bad, can't be overstated.

THRESHOLD RITUALS

How you cross spaces matters. What you do when walking into a boardroom or through your front door at night sets the tone for what follows. A simple breath, a posture reset, or even a change of shoes can mark the shift. Small threshold rituals prevent one environment from contaminating another.

FREEDOM THROUGH DESIGN

Energy is the currency. Emotions are the signal. The environment is the lever.

Most people ignore the lever because it seems invisible. You can't grit your way out of a toxic environment. You can only design your way out. Learn to shape your settings—physical, digital, relational—and you'll free up capacity you didn't know you had.

This strategy isn't about control for control's sake. It's about freedom. Freedom to show up with clarity instead of noise. Freedom to choose how you enter a room instead of leaking stress into it. Freedom to create a setting where trust, rather than fear, can grow.

TAKING CONTROL

One of the simplest ways to take control of your environment is through your body.

I've learned this most clearly by working with kids—both my own and hundreds of junior athletes. When they'd start spinning out—too much energy, too little focus—we'd hit pause for a breathing or movement break. Ten deep breaths, legs up on the couch, or a few quick drills. Just a quick reset. Soon, they started doing it on their own. Parents would call asking, "What did you do to my kid? He's watching TV and suddenly starts doing push-ups during the commercials!" Those kids were learning how to manage their energy before it managed them.

The same pattern works for professionals. Before a big test, a match, or a business meeting, movement and breath can shift your entire state. I once coached a young entrepreneur who loved boxing, so I created a simple pre-meeting flow for him: a few cross-body movements to wake up his system, two minutes of long exhales, a minute of box breathing, and then a few sharp breaths to bring his focus back up just before he walked in.

I chose cross-body movements because anything that crosses the midline of the body helps activate attention and sharpen focus.

Reaching, twisting, or throwing light punches across the body wakes up both sides of the brain and pulls you into the present moment. The long exhales helped settle his nervous system and quiet the noise. Box breathing—equal time inhaling, holding, exhaling, and holding—helped stabilize that calmer state. And the sharp breaths at the end made sure he didn't walk in flat or underenergized, but alert, present, and ready to execute.

That small ritual steadied his body, cleared his mind, and sharpened his presence. It's the same structure I've used with athletes heading into finals and executives heading into negotiations.

Calmness and sharpness aren't opposites—they're partners. The body is the switchboard. Once you know how to use it, you can reset any environment from the inside out.

ENVIRONMENTAL LAYERING

When it comes to our outer environment, it's easy to think of it as the background: the walls, the lights, the gear. But in performance, the environment is not passive—it's active. It shapes behavior in real time. It holds memory. It tells the body how to show up before the brain even kicks in. And if you know how to layer it right, it does half the coaching for you.

That's what I teach—environmental layering. It's the difference between just being in a room and having the room work for you. You want every layer of that space doing a job: stabilizing energy, triggering readiness, reinforcing rhythm. Not one layer. All of them.

LAYER 1: PHYSICAL CUES

Start with the obvious. The layout, the flow, the lighting, the sound. None of that is aesthetic fluff; it's all signal.

In elite performance spaces, everything you see and touch is telling your nervous system something. Is the room chaotic or clean? Are the materials haphazard or intentional? Does the setup guide you toward focused effort—or make you scramble to figure out what's next?

In a gym, it's about the setup. Are the tools in the right place? Are transitions smooth? Is the warm-up zone pulling people into readiness, or are they wandering in cold and distracted? When I work with coaches, we design warm-ups like launch pads—not just for the body, but for the brain. And this applies far beyond sports. In corporate environments, where's the reset space? Where's the quiet zone between meetings? Where does your body know *This is where we shift gears, drop distractions, and recenter?* Designing performance means removing friction. Every bit of friction costs attention. And attention is your most valuable resource.

LAYER 2: EMOTIONAL CUES

This one is sneakier. Emotional cues don't come from motivational posters hung on the wall. They come from tone, language, what's allowed to happen—and what isn't.

In high-functioning teams, emotional cues are intentional. The music in the locker room before a match. The silence before a meeting starts. The breath you take before a lift. These all prime the system, but emotional cues can also backfire. If you let anxiety go unchecked, that becomes the emotional tone. If people use sarcasm to dodge real conversations, that becomes the cue. If you celebrate loudness and ignore presence, you teach people that noise matters more than connection.

I once worked with a team that couldn't figure out why their Monday meetings always started scattered. The energy was always off, and focus was hard to recover. Turns out, everyone walked in five minutes late, heads down, with their phones out. No eye contact. No transition.

We changed one thing. We built a two-minute transition ritual that put the phones down and answered one question: What are you bringing into the room today? That cue alone changed the opening beat of every week. The system recalibrated.

LAYER 3: IDENTITY CUES

This is where it gets powerful. If you want to change behavior, you don't just need a different action—you need a different identity. The environment can help anchor that. You use the space to whisper to the nervous system: This is who you are when you're here.

A championship locker room doesn't just have towels and benches. It has history. Symbols. Rituals. You don't step in there casually. The room says: This matters. That weight helps performers drop in faster, go deeper, and recover cleaner. So, when I walk into a gym, I ask, What identity does this place reinforce? Is this a room for grinders and warriors? Or victims and show ponies?

I've been in facilities with seven-figure budgets and zero soul. State-of-the-art equipment. No grit. No glue. And I've been in garages where the walls were cracked, the mats were worn thin—but the culture ran deep. Because someone had built the room with meaning. Layer by layer.

Remember, environments can either cost you energy or contribute to it. They either make your job harder or easier. The average coach tries to force culture through motivation. The elite coach designs culture into the room (more on that later).

And the same principle applies to how you set up your day. Your calendar is an environment. Your desktop is an environment. Your social circle is an environment. Every layer you control is a vote for how your system shows up. So, start asking: What are the cues in your world actually training you to do? Whether you see it or not, you are always being trained. And the environment is either a silent liability or your most trusted performance partner.

ENVIRONMENT AS LEADERSHIP

I believe that leadership reveals itself first through the air in a room. You can feel it before you see it—the tone, the temperature, the way people breathe. Walk into a locker room after a loss, a boardroom before a firing, or a family dinner when someone's said too much, and you know within seconds what kind of world you've entered. The air carries its own kind of truth. It tells you what's allowed, what's feared, and what's waiting to be said.

Some rooms hum. You can hear it in the small sounds—the shuffle of papers, the rhythm of footsteps, the way conversations start and stop without breaking trust. There's movement even in silence, a sense that energy is flowing in the right direction. Other rooms are still. The air feels thin. People speak carefully, like every sentence is being weighed, and even the light seems colder. What fascinates me is that the difference is rarely about the people themselves. It's about the space those people have been given to exist in—and that, more often than not, comes down to the leader.

Years ago, I worked with a team that had everything a coach could ask for: talent, resources, ambition. But the environment was off. You could hear the tension in the hallways before practice, a kind of static that hummed beneath even the best intentions. Nobody trusted that what they said in the locker room would stay there. Meetings were sharp and efficient but left everyone a little smaller than when they'd walked in. It wasn't strategy that was missing; it was safety. The air was heavy, and no one could quite breathe.

That was the first time I understood how much a leader's

presence shapes chemistry. When the conditions are right, people move better, think more clearly, and recover more quickly. When they're wrong, even the best performers tighten up. The formula isn't complicated—space shapes state, state drives behavior, and behavior compounds into results. But leading inside that chain takes an awareness that most people never practice. It requires noticing the invisible.

The best leaders I've known don't try to control people. They shape the conditions around them until the desired behavior becomes almost inevitable. They don't demand trust; they design for it. They don't preach focus; they build rooms where focus happens naturally. You can see it in how they start a meeting—not by asserting authority, but by clearing space. You can feel it in how they handle tension. They don't pass it along like static electricity; they ground it. They regulate the atmosphere so others can stay steady.

I used to think leadership was pressure. The louder, harder, faster kind that pushes people into action. But pressure without structure doesn't produce strength—it creates distortion. It bends people into compliance instead of commitment. Real leadership builds the structure first, then applies the right amount of weight. You can tell the difference instantly. When a team walks into a well-designed environment, they don't brace. They expand. The shoulders roll back. The tone deepens. The room breathes.

Every leader carries their own weather system. It's invisible but constant. Some bring storms that roll in without warning; others carry droughts where nothing grows. But the great ones? They understand the climate they create. They show up with consistency, not perfection, and they know how to steady the temperature when the air starts to shift. They realize that everyone in the room is calibrating off their energy, whether they mean to or not.

I ask leaders one question when I start working with them: What's it like to work in your weather? Most have never thought about it. They know their goals, their values, their metrics, but not the texture of their presence—the way a room feels when they walk in, or what's left behind when they leave. That's where culture actually lives. Not in documents or slogans, but in the air people breathe while trying to do their best work.

People learn faster in rooms that breathe. They take risks in spaces that hold them. They find rhythm when the leader holds the rhythm first. That's why the best leadership often looks like absence. The leader has shaped the environment so completely that their influence becomes invisible, absorbed into the system itself. The team just functions, clean and confident, as if the room itself knows what to do.

Think of leadership as architecture. It's the quiet work of arranging space, tone, and trust until the air starts teaching on its own. And once that happens, you don't have to shout. You don't have to chase. You can walk into any room, take a breath, and know that the work you've done—the work no one sees—is already speaking for you.

CREATING OPTIMAL WORK ENVIRONMENTS

When I was running a club in Melbourne, I hired a young guy named Mike. He didn't have the right résumé, didn't tick the boxes corporate cared about. My boss told me not to take him. "He's not experienced enough," he said. But something about the way Mike carried himself caught my attention. He didn't talk like a salesperson trying to convince me he was the right fit. He talked like someone who actually saw people. He had a quiet sincerity about him.

I hired him anyway. Two months later, he was the best salesperson in the building. He spent more time on the floor than at his desk, walking through the gym, checking in with members, remembering minor details about their lives. He met people where they were.

Every day, someone would come in asking for him. Every week, his numbers outpaced everyone else's. At first, the other managers hated it—he wasn't making the required number of calls, wasn't logging enough follow-ups. But his results spoke for themselves. The members he signed up didn't just join; they stayed. That was the metric that mattered most.

Watching him changed how I thought about leadership. I stopped managing behavior and started managing environments. My job wasn't to force everyone into the same mold. It was to figure out what kind of space each person needed to perform their best and then create just enough structure for them to stretch without breaking.

Not everyone was like Mike. I had another salesperson who couldn't stand the noise of the gym floor. She liked numbers and order, spreadsheets and schedules. The idea of stopping someone mid-workout to pitch a membership made her uncomfortable. But give her a list of renewals to call through in the back office, and she'd crush it. So that's where I put her.

At the time, I didn't think of it as a philosophy. I was just trying to keep the place running. But looking back, I realize that's where I first learned how an environment drives performance. When people are working against their nature, you can feel it—the air tightens, their energy flattens, the small problems start to multiply. But when they're in the right spot, it's like the whole system breathes easier.

That's what happened with Mike. Once he found his rhythm, the entire club found it with him. The energy shifted. The culture followed. Members stayed longer, the team got tighter, and we started hitting targets that used to feel out of reach.

I've thought about that lesson a lot since then, especially when I'm coaching athletes or executives who feel stuck. They're burned out because they're out of alignment—doing good work in the wrong environment, pushing their system in the wrong direction. The longer you stay in a space that doesn't fit, the more it costs you.

That club taught me that leadership is about calibration. You find the rhythm of each person and adjust the environment until the team starts to move as one. It's the same thing martial arts taught me on the mat—you can't force a move that doesn't fit the body. You find the leverage that's already there. You make space for flow. And when you do it right, you don't have to motivate people anymore. The environment does it for you.

ENVIRONMENTAL REDESIGN

Here's the thing about your environment: It's louder than you think. Walk into your own space and really look. The pile on your desk, the unopened emails, the half-dead plant, the way your phone never shuts up. Each one is a thief. Small crimes, constant noise.

That's the real drain.

You can't out-discipline chaos. You have to design around it. Here's a way to do it.

STEP 1: PICK YOUR ZONE

Forget about balance. Start with the one thing that pisses you off most. The corner you avoid. The app that eats your mornings. The conversation that leaves you feeling like you just boxed 12 rounds with a ghost. That's your zone. That's where the system's leaking.

STEP 2: FIND THE FRICTION

Don't overthink it. Just listen. What feels off? What makes you grind your teeth? What do you keep promising to fix "when things slow down"?

STEP 3: CHANGE ONE LEVER

Do something about the friction. Move the desk. Close the damn tab. Mute the chat. Tell the person what's not working instead of pretending it is, or take a breath and choose silence instead of reaction. Silence can be a weapon too. Make one change: small, clean, immediate.

STEP 4: RUN THE 3-3-3 RULE

Three small fixes each week for three weeks.

That's it. Forget the charts and apps. Just start moving again.

STEP 5: WATCH WHAT HAPPENS

Your body will tell you first. Sleep comes easier. Focus sticks longer. You stop snapping at the people who don't deserve it. You'll notice when the noise creeps back in—because peace, once you've had it, gets addictive.

Energy is the currency. Emotions are the signal. Your environment is the lever. Most people ignore the lever because it feels invisible. But it's the fastest one to pull. You can't grit your way out of a toxic environment. You can only design your way out. Shape your settings—physical, digital, relational—and you free up capacity you didn't know you had.

When your environment stops being something you manage and instead becomes something you embody, it's not simply external. It's woven into how you move through the world.

That's what the next chapter is about—the spiral. Because once you've aligned your energy, regulated your emotions, and shaped your environment, you still have to navigate the part that never stops moving: the cycle itself.

Chapter Six

THE SPIRAL

I've spent a lot of time in airport parking garages. That's the job—jumping from one country to the next, coaching someone through a match in Tokyo, then flying straight to Madrid, then Melbourne, then back to L.A. And in all that travel, I started noticing something. Every garage feels the same. Same concrete. Same low ceilings. Same dim lights.

And always the same spiral.

You circle up. You circle down. You miss a turn, and you're back where you started. You follow signs that promise open spaces but they're wrong or already filled. Sometimes you drive around endlessly, second-guessing whether you're even going in the right direction.

THE PARKING GARAGE OF PERFORMANCE

The experience of navigating airport parking garages is like your Pressure Code. Often, you think you're gaining altitude, but you're just circling the same floor. You keep chasing momentum, but it loops you back into old habits. And then, sometimes, you're technically climbing, but emotionally, you're out of gas. The worst part? When you're in the garage, often you can't tell if you're spiraling up or spiraling down.

The performance spiral is real, and unfortunately, most try to escape it by hitting the accelerator. Which just means more driving around, more noise, more chaos, and burning through your fuel even faster! Or they simply stop. They're parked and idling without a map, no sense of direction, and unsure of where they even are. Getting to the next performance level? A complete mystery. So, they pull over, pull the brake, and shut down.

I used to think spiraling was just a metaphor—what people said when someone was emotionally tanking or couldn't hold it together under pressure. But then I noticed it was showing up everywhere. In how the body moves, how the brain stores memory, the way time doesn't really feel linear, especially when you're under stress.

Spirals are a pattern. Your muscles contract in spirals. Your DNA is encoded in a spiral. Even the earth isn't circling the sun on a flat track—it's moving forward through space in a long, layered spiral sometimes called the solar spiral or galactic spiral model. The seasons loop as well, but they also push you forward.

That's what performance feels like when it's working. It repeats, but it evolves.

The same holds true when it's not working, and the pressure collapses your code. Spirals are simply what they are—they aren't inherently good or bad. They're how systems move, which means you're never truly standing still. You're either spiraling up and gaining awareness, clarity, and recovery, or spiraling down and leaking energy, misfiring emotions, and repeating patterns that don't serve you anymore.

Like our parking garage metaphor, you can waste a lot of time circling the same level, convinced you're making progress. And when you do make your way back to the ramp? Down is the easy path. Up takes more effort. Yes, the parking garage is designed to lead you to the exits without you having to think about them. But you're not looking for the exit. You don't want to spiral down. You want to climb!

THE COST OF THE DOWNWARD SPIRAL

Aryna didn't recognize her own downward spiral at first. From the outside, she looked like she was on track—deep tournament runs, big headlines, a Slam win under her belt. But inside, she was circling. Each match felt heavier than the last. Her recovery got sloppy. Her team dynamics were loose. Emotionally, she was grinding instead of growing.

At Indian Wells, Arnya lost the final to 17-year-old Mirra Andreeva. It wasn't the kind of result that tanks a season, but it rattled her confidence. Then, in Stuttgart, it wasn't even close. Straight sets, 6-4, 6-1, to an unseeded opponent. She was out of rhythm; the cracks in her system were on display.

At Roland-Garros, the pattern tightened. She took the first set off Coco Gauff in a tie-break. But when Gauff steadied in the second, Aryna unraveled. Her posture shifted. Her breathing changed. She dropped the third set 6-4.

Then came Wimbledon. The pressure, the press, the surface—everything felt heavier. The signs showed up in Arnya's shoulder. A nagging injury that came from thousands of swings stacked under pressure. After the loss to Anisimova, she sat in the media room and said, "Losing sucks. You always feel like you want to die . . ."

Spirals accumulate over time. Aryna's recovery windows were shrinking, and her rituals between points were disappearing. She was still winning matches, so she didn't adjust her training or lighten her emotional load. And that's the trap top performers face. When you're good enough to win while spiraling down, the results lie to you. They cover the cracks. But your system knows. Your body knows. You lose sharpness. You start reacting instead of choosing, and everything becomes harder than it should be.

I worked with a founder who was sharp and charismatic, all gas and no brakes. He was splitting his time between L.A., Austin, and New York, landing big clients, making headlines, and raising capital. On paper, he was flying. But in real life? He was unraveling. He had gut issues, brain fog, and a tightness in his chest that wouldn't go away. His calendar was booked to the minute, his diet was garbage, and he hadn't taken a real breath in months.

His downward spiral had already started; he just didn't recognize it yet. He thought more movement would fix it. That the next win would reset him. But he was stuck on that parking garage floor, hitting the gas and feeling like he was going places.

In the spiral, it's easy to misdiagnose speed as assent, burning through the gas while making little to no progress toward your destination. And it doesn't hit all at once. It wears you down until you're out of position, out of rhythm, and out of trust—with yourself, your process, and your team.

SPIRAL UP VERSUS SPIRAL DOWN

The spiral doesn't care which way you're going. It simply amplifies whatever system you're running. If you're reactive, scattered, burned out, and emotionally leaky, the spiral will drag you down faster than you can recover.

But when you're aligned, regulated, and clear, the spiral lifts you. You still meet the same pressure, the same fear, the same moments that test you—but now you see them sooner. Decisions come faster. Action follows immediately. You're not guessing or forcing it; you're executing from a place of understanding, confidence, and trust in your system.

Whether you go up or down depends on how well you manage your inputs. The more you align your energy, your emotions, and your environment, the more that spiral becomes your lift, not your leak. That's when momentum actually makes an impact.

NEW APPS ON THE OPERATING SYSTEM

Things started shifting for Aryna when she started driving her own growth. When you're stuck, it's tempting to reach for a new app. A new tool, a new book, a new breathwork technique. Something that feels fresh. And to be clear—those things can help. Like any app you install, they can enhance, refine, and expand what you do. But they can't run the system for you. What creates *sustained* lift through the spiral isn't any app. It's the quality of the Pressure Code itself—finding the sweet spot where your energy, emotions, and environment are in harmony and working together. It's the loop, zooming in and zooming out, and then stepping back and examining it all again.

After the French Open, when we were in Berlin, Aryna showed up to our first practice and shared questions she was wrestling with and the things she wanted to understand about herself. She didn't want to just practice her swing or work on her form; she wanted to dig deeper and understand her system.

I didn't give her an answer or a quick fix. We talked, but there were no prescriptions or tactics. It was just clarity about her internal environment and how that was affecting her emotionally and draining her energy. That's how you get out of a downward spiral, by learning to see the system and making space for real reflection. It means being honest with yourself, mustering the courage to let the fears out of your head so they can stop owning you.

That marked the beginning of Aryna's upward turn. It wasn't a perfect climb—there were still setbacks—but her mindset changed. Yes, she absolutely had a new app or two running. But her operating system had come back into alignment and was working for her again.

THE POWER OF THE MIRROR

I want to bring up something that is key. There's a moment in every performance journey where you have to *stop* moving. Not for long. And not because you're tired or done. But because motion can lie to you. And if you're not careful, you'll mistake momentum for meaning. You'll be grinding hard, checking boxes, winning games, but something inside you will feel fractured. Off. Like you're not really in sync with the work anymore.

The results look fine on paper. But behind the scenes, the system is unraveling. Energy's leaking. Emotional resilience is thin. You'll reach for new tools, but the foundation isn't holding because you're building on self-deception instead of truth.

Self-deception is seductive. It's protective. It tells you what you want to hear: "You're fine." "This is just a rough patch." "You just need to push harder." But your body knows. Your relationships know. Your clarity fades, and your decisions get foggy. You snap quicker. You spiral.

If you want real, sustainable, improved performance, you have to get honest. You need to be completely, often brutally honest with yourself. So stop what you're doing, take a step back, and take a hard look in the mirror. See what's *objectively* happening. This won't be easy work. It demands that you put down the performance mask and ask the questions that actually matter. Questions like:

Where am I avoiding truth in the name of progress?

What's the cost of the story I'm telling myself right now?

Who am I blaming instead of owning it myself?

Most people never slow down long enough to ask those questions. They're afraid of the answers and afraid of the emptiness. They're afraid they won't like the reflection they see. But it's not the mirror that breaks you. It's refusing to look.

Honesty is not weakness or pessimism. It's not a detour from growth—it *is* growth. It's what recalibrates the system. Honesty is clarity. And without it, the tools, reps, and frameworks won't work. That's why your Pressure Code isn't *just* about performance—it's about becoming. And you can't become what you won't acknowledge.

So, the question is simple: Are you willing to be honest with yourself? Not once. Not when it's convenient. But as a way of life? If you are, you can stop spiraling downward and start ascending.

I once worked with a leader named Chase. From the outside, he had everything dialed in—background, body, balance sheet. But inside, he was brittle. He knew it; he just didn't want to face it. He kept trying to optimize his way out of the discomfort. New apps. New hacks. Better scheduling. More breathwork. But none of it worked. His spiral was systematic, and his code was failing under pressure.

The moment it started to change for Chase was the moment he got honest and acknowledged that his system wasn't working, that the version of success he was chasing was starting to cost him more than it was worth. That moment of clarity didn't solve everything, but it gave him the insight to know where to begin.

That's the only way to exit the loop. You can't force your way out, and you can't exit a spiral that you refuse to see. The only way to step out of a downward spiral and into the next level of performance is through clarity and honesty.

DEFEND, CONTROL, ATTACK

Let's break this down to make it useful. I learned this sequence from my jiujitsu coach, Jhunior Guarnido: defend, control, attack. While this sequence is focused on combat sports, it goes beyond fighting. Under pressure, most people struggle because they act too soon. They try to win before they're stable. When that happens, they risk spiraling in the wrong direction.

DEFEND

Defend comes first for a reason. Instead of reacting to every thought or signal in the environment, you defend your energy and emotional state, never letting the situation take more from you than it should. Starting with defense means starting from a position of strength. Your posture is steady, and your breathing is slow and controlled. You have no obvious openings or unnecessary leaks. Your attention isn't scattered but sharp and focused. When you defend well, pressure has to work to break through and reach you.

CONTROL

Once you're stable and aligned, you can shift into control and decide where your energy goes. You decide what matters and what doesn't. You adjust your position—physically, mentally, emotionally—so you have leverage. Control is about seeking alignment, not domination. You're aware of yourself. You're aware of what's happening around you. You're no longer just inside the moment but oriented within it. With control and alignment, you can channel your momentum toward an upward spiral. Only then does attacking make sense.

ATTACK

An attack is when you execute. It's action without hesitation. It's not rushed or emotional, but rather clean and direct. When you attack from a controlled position, you don't waste energy proving anything. You apply pressure where it belongs and only for as long as it's needed. And if something slips—if timing is off or resistance shows up—you don't panic. You cycle back. You defend again. You regain control. You keep spiraling upward.

When people reverse the order, it starts the downward spiral. They attack from frustration. They push from exhaustion. They force outcomes from a compromised state. Their effort feels intense, but it's unstable. It burns fuel fast and creates the illusion of progress while quietly draining the system.

Upward spirals move differently. They're quieter. More deliberate. They respect the sequence. Defend first. Then control. Then act. And when pressure hits hard, the fastest way back to defense—the quickest way to stop leaking energy and regain position—is through your body, which brings us back to breathing.

BREATHING

You have a superpower that will travel into the spiral with you—and that's your breath! Yes, we're back to breathing again because I can't overstate how powerful it is. I preach it so much I often get asked where it all started. Did I go to a seminar? Travel to India and study with a guru in the jungle? Pick it up from a book?

If you haven't figured it out by now, my understanding was initially forged through my lived experience as a child navigating a tough and unforgiving world. This was not a traditional education, I know. But it was powerful and life-changing. So, let me go back to the moment it started for me.

I was 11, standing at my father's military funeral. The guns went off, and the soldiers, adorned in their dress uniforms, folded the flag. I watched it move through my mother's hands and then into mine. I can still remember the feel of the fabric as I clutched it, and my aunt's grip on my shoulders.

And that's the moment. Suddenly, in the middle of all that noise and ceremony, I noticed something no one had ever taught me about: my breath. Because I knew if I let it go, I'd lose it. So I focused on breathing . . . slow and steady, trying to keep from breaking down. And it grounded me. It placed me in control despite the world spinning around me. I grabbed hold of that feeling like the anchor it was. In and out. It tethered me against the raging storm.

That was the first time I realized that my breath could change how I felt.

Years later, every martial arts class began and ended with breathing. There was no music or talking, just the quiet sound of our breaths. We'd kneel, eyes closed, clearing the noise, narrowing our focus. Then, without warning, Sensei would clap twice—boom—and we'd explode into the warm-up: calisthenics, fire drills, grappling, and sparring. The rule was simple: Breathe and move. No sound, no complaining, no reaction. Even when you got hit, even when the coach smacked you mid-sparring to test your focus—you kept breathing.

That experience at the funeral and subsequent training wired me differently. Breathing was more than recovery; it was control. We'd finish class lying flat on our backs, arms out, palms up, breathing slowly—each exhale a little longer than the last.

That's where I learned the foundation of everything I teach today: Train the body to control the mind.

It's what got me off the streets. It's what made me calm under pressure. It's what every elite performer needs. Once you can control your body, you can control your state. And once you can control your state, you can control your journey along the spiral.

Yes, I talk about breathing often in this book. I even suggest different ways and techniques. So, let's just pause and get to the basics for a moment. I don't care where you are, what you're doing, or if you're spiraling up or aimlessly circling the same damn parking garage. You can *always* breathe. Because if you're not breathing, well, you're dead.

I want you to try it a little differently as well. Breathe *in through* the nose and *out through* the nose. I know, you've maybe been taught to exhale through your mouth. There's some faster up-regulating where that will definitely come into play, but right now, what we want is *nasal* breathing and breath holds.

Breath is that physical, tangible thing that you have control over and will give you control back. Regardless of how you're feeling, breathwork will allow you to bring yourself to the state that's needed to perform your best. To allow you to use pressure as fuel instead of as an obstacle or resistance. Breath allows you to decide to take an action regardless of what's going on around you.

But beyond my describing it to you or convincing you how vital it is, you're going to have to apply it. So, the real heavy lifting in this chapter has been moved to the appendix at the back of the book. There you'll find more breathing exercises as well as a QR code that will take you to additional online tools and resources. This will give you the steps, regardless of where you're at in the spiral, to get back to your breath. To take control so that when the pressure hits your code, you'll be poised to spiral up instead of down.

Chapter Seven

BUILDING YOUR PRESSURE CODE

When I met Aryna, she was all fire without direction. She had everything—power, hunger, drive, pure f*cking energy. It made her dangerous on the court, but it was uncontrolled, wild. It went everywhere and nowhere. If it worked, she didn't know why. If it didn't, she had no idea how to fix it.

She was a monster. And she hadn't learned how to harness her fire yet.

That's where most people get stuck. They think the goal is to become something they're not. Calmer. More disciplined. Less emotional. But that's bullshit. You are who you are. The fire inside you—that hunger, that intensity—that's not the problem. The problem is you're letting it run your system instead of directing it.

Becoming a warrior isn't about killing the fighter inside you. It's about learning how to harness that beast. How to direct that energy. How to build a system that lets you use everything you've got without burning yourself to the ground. But you don't need to be competing on the world's stage to see how this plays out.

I once worked with an entrepreneur named Tom who was about to walk into the biggest lunch of his career. The meeting would decide whether his new coaching business lived or died. Before that day, Tom had done what most ambitious people do: studied every tactic, sales script, and negotiation framework. He memorized natural language processing phrasing and body language cues. He knew all the "apps." But his operating system was crashing underneath.

He'd show up at important meetings jittery and distracted. He'd fumble through his own words, trying to look confident, but his energy told the opposite story. He had his own kind of fire burning, and it wasn't serving him.

So instead of adding another trick, we stripped everything back. I gave him one task: breathe. Every time the other person talked, Tom would focus on keeping a steady rhythm and building awareness. He wasn't trying to *seem* calm anymore; he *was* calm. The confidence people felt from him shifted from rehearsed to real. His attention was anchored, his arousal levels balanced, and his energy clear.

That lunch changed the course of his business. Within the span of a year, he'd scaled to a full coaching company, bought his dream car, and built a team that trusted him. Not because of the tactics—those remained the same. What changed was the person running them. That's what the Pressure Code does. It doesn't replace skill; it allows your skills to *work*. And that's what this chapter is about.

THE PERSON WHO GOT YOU HERE

After Wimbledon, Aryna showed up in Berlin differently. She walked onto the court and immediately started talking—not about her shots, but about the books she'd been reading, the questions she was wrestling with, and the things she'd always kept locked in her head.

She wanted to return to the fundamentals we'd built years ago. But she no longer wanted them purely for performance. The breathing work, the reset rituals, and the awareness tools that helped her stay grounded when everything around her demanded elite performance—she wanted them for *everything.* And that's when I knew something in her had shifted. She was no longer trying to fix what was broken; she was trying to become someone who could sustain what she'd built.

There's a difference between obtaining success and sustaining it. Obtaining success is about grinding, pushing, and doing whatever it takes to reach the goal. The person who gets you there is the fighter—someone willing to bleed, to claw, and to show up when it hurts. But sustaining success is about character. It's about your identity and becoming someone whose system can hold the weight of winning without collapsing under the pressure. The person who got you here needs to become the person who keeps you here.

TWO KINDS OF FEAR

Most people think success is about overcoming fear. But that's only half true. There are two kinds of fear.

THE FEAR OF LOSING

This is the obvious one.

It's the fear that drives you onto the court, into the gym, and through the pain. This can be useful to keep you moving, but it's shallow. Because at the end of the day, you're still running *from* something instead of *toward* something. This fear makes you a fighter, but fighters burn out.

THE FEAR OF FACING YOURSELF

This is the deeper one.

It's the fear that keeps you grinding the same way even when it's not working. It's the fear that makes you avoid the hard questions. It's the fear that stops you from addressing the thing you know you need to fix because fixing it might break you. Aryna had this fear with her serve until that crucial day in San Jose.

The fear that matters most isn't the fear of losing. It's the fear of looking at yourself in the mirror, with brutal honesty, and admitting what needs to change.

THE THREE BIG QUESTIONS

When Aryna came to me in Berlin asking to rebuild her system, I didn't hand her a new routine or give her a pep talk. I asked her three questions. These are the same three questions I ask every athlete, executive, and elite performer I work with. They're simple, but they will cut through everything:

- What works well?
- What needs work?
- What's the plan?

WHAT WORKS WELL?

Not what *used to* work. Not what you *think* should work. What is *actually working* right now? Most people skip this step. They're so focused on fixing what's broken that they forget to protect what's already strong. But if you don't know what's working, you can't build on it. With Aryna, it was her intensity—her fire. It was her competitive edge that made her dangerous. We weren't trying to kill that but to channel it.

WHAT NEEDS WORK?

This is where real honesty matters. When you need to ask yourself the hard questions. What's actually broken? What are you avoiding? What are you pretending is fine when it's not? For Aryna, it was emotional regulation, energy management, her relationship with high-pressure environments like Wimbledon, and the serve she was too scared to touch.

WHAT'S THE PLAN?

What are you going to do *this week* to address what needs work? The plan has to be specific and objective. It has to be something you have complete control over and something you'll do regardless of the outcome. That's where most people fail. They make vague commitments like, "I'll work harder." "I'll focus more." "I'll be better."

That's not a plan. A plan is: "I'll run the reset loop twice a day for seven days." "I'll track my energy deposits and leaks in a notebook." "I'll practice one breathing drill before every high-stakes moment." Concrete. Controllable. Clear.

THE FOUR BIG QUALIFIERS

Once you have your plan, run it through these four qualifiers. If it doesn't meet all four, it's not actually a plan, and you need to go back and rework it.

IT IS EXTREMELY OBJECTIVE

Can someone else verify whether you did it or not?

"I'll be more present" is subjective. "I'll put my phone on airplane mode during my takeoff blocks" is objective.

IT IS SOMETHING I HAVE 100% CONTROL OVER

You can't control outcomes. You can't control other people. You can't control the weather or the crowd or whether your opponent shows up having the best day of their life. But you can control your preparatic [illegible] abits, and your response.

IT IS HIGHLY SPECIFIC

Not "I'll manage my energy better," but "I'll schedule a 30-minute takeoff block every morning at 8 AM." "I'll walk for 15 minutes after lunch." "I'll run a descent ritual at 6 PM." Specificity removes any ambiguity.

I WILL DO THIS REGARDLESS OF THE OUTCOME

This is the hardest one. Most people only stick to their system when it's working, when they're winning and the motivation comes easily. But the system is what carries you when you lose and your motivation fades. That's your code under pressure.

If your commitment is conditional, it's not a system.

THE CHARACTER GROWTH ASSESSMENT

Here's where it gets deeper. The Three Big Questions tell you *what* to do. The Four Big Qualifiers ensure you'll *actually* do it. But the

Character Growth Assessment tells you *who you need to become* to sustain it.

The most sustainable way to raise your capacity is to deepen your character. Hard work is great. But the goal here is to become someone who can consistently handle the load. To do so, ask yourself the following questions.

QUESTION 1: WHO DO YOU NEED TO BECOME TO ACCOMPLISH THIS?

This question doesn't ask what skills you need or what tactics. It asks, *Who* do you need to be?

For Aryna, it wasn't about becoming a better tennis player. She was already elite. She needed to become someone who could regulate emotions under pressure. Someone who could manage energy across a grueling season. Someone who could walk into hostile environments and stay grounded.

QUESTION 2: WHAT WOULD FUTURE YOU DO IN THIS SCENARIO?

This one forces perspective. When you're in the moment—tired, frustrated, doubting yourself—it's easy to default to old patterns. But if you imagine the version of yourself who's already solved this problem, what would they do? Would they skip the breathing drill because they're too tired? Would they avoid the hard conversation? Would they let the downward spiral start?

No. Future you would do the hard thing, every time.

QUESTION 3: WHAT IS THE THING YOU KNOW YOU SHOULD DO, BUT SCARES YOU THE MOST?

This is the one people avoid because, deep down, you already know what needs to happen. You're just afraid to face it. For Aryna, it was her serve. For a leader I worked with, it was setting boundaries with his CEO. For the founder spiraling into burnout, it was admitting his company culture was toxic. The thing that scares you most is usually the thing holding you back. And the only way out is through.

IT DOESN'T MATTER HOW YOU FEEL

One of the things I drilled into Aryna for years—it was basically a mantra—was this: It doesn't matter how you feel.

You have to be fresh enough to perform. You have to be ready enough to compete. But how you *feel* right now? That's not the deciding factor. Because if you wait until you feel great to do the thing, you'll wait forever. Nobody always feels great. Nobody wakes up every day lit up and ready. Some days you're flat. Some days you're off. Some days everything in your body is telling you to stay in bed.

Do the thing anyway.

Not recklessly. Not ignoring real signals. But understanding that action comes before the feeling—not after. You don't feel confident and then perform. You perform, and confidence follows. You don't feel motivated and then train. You train, and motivation catches up.

I tell people this all the time: If you need everything to be perfect before you can perform your best, then you're not ready yet. It's not meant as an insult; it's the skill gap.

Champions don't wait for the right feeling or the right conditions—they've trained themselves to create the state they need through action. They don't rely on alignment; they manufacture it. If the room is off, they steady themselves. If the body feels flat, they move it. If the mind is noisy, they narrow their focus and execute anyway.

Most people wait for the feeling to do the thing. The most resilient performers do the thing to generate the feeling—knowing the feeling itself was never the goal. Action is.

This isn't about grinding through pain for the sake of it. It's about building something deeper: the identity of someone who executes regardless of conditions.

Every time you show up when you don't feel like it, you're telling yourself a story. You're adding evidence to a belief: *I'm the kind of person who gets it done.* That belief compounds. Over time, it becomes unshakable. You walk into any room knowing—not hoping, *knowing*—that you can handle it. Maybe it won't be perfect. But you'll handle it.

I've had moments where I went in feeling terrible—tired, sick, distracted—and it turned out to be one of my best performances. Why? Because I wasn't carrying the pressure of needing it to be great. I just showed up and let it happen.

And I've had moments where everything was lined up perfectly, and I still fell flat. That's the game.

The point is this: Feelings lie. They're weather, not climate. If you let them dictate your actions, you'll be at the mercy of something you can't control. But if you act first—if you do the thing regardless—you take back control.

Clarity, control, awareness. These don't come from perfect conditions. They come from proving to yourself, over and over, that conditions don't own you.

That's one of the most important skills you can develop. Not the breathing drills or the resets or the energy audits—though those matter. The deeper skill is this: knowing you can perform even when you don't feel like performing. That's what makes the system unbreakable.

THE PEAK PERFORMANCE TIMELINE

Now we get tactical.

You've identified what works, what needs work, and what the plan is. You've run it through the qualifiers. You've done the character work. Now you need to map it to your calendar. This is what I call the peak performance timeline. It's how you reverse-engineer your energy investments so you peak when it matters most.

TIME YOUR ENERGY SO YOU PEAK WHEN YOU NEED IT

Most people spend energy randomly. They go hard every day. They treat every meeting, every workout, every moment like it's the championship. Then, when the actual moment comes—the final, the pitch, the negotiation—they're already depleted. The goal should be to build your schedule so that your energy, emotions, and environment align at the moments that matter most.

STEP 1: IDENTIFY YOUR PEAK MOMENTS

When do you need to be at your absolute best? For Aryna, it's the Grand Slam. For an executive, it might be quarterly board meetings. For a founder, it's the product launch or fundraising round. For a parent, it may be helping a child with their homework after an already long day. Mark those on your calendar. Everything else will build toward those moments.

STEP 2: BUILD YOUR ENERGY RHYTHM

Work backward from your peak moments. Let's go back to our flight metaphor:

- Takeoff blocks: 30–60 minutes of full intensity. No distractions with maximum output. These are where you focus your energy.

- Cruise blocks: 60–90 minutes of steady work, keeping an efficient rhythm. These are where you sustain your energy.
- Descent blocks: 20–30 minutes to close loops, reset, and recover. These are where you protect your energy.

The exact timing will vary depending on the task and the person, but the rhythm stays the same. It's a short, intense takeoff to get airborne, a longer, efficient cruise where the work flows, and a deliberate descent before fatigue and noise creep in.

Most people live in a permanent takeoff. You need to cycle your energy so you don't burn out before the moments that actually matter.

STEP 3: AUDIT YOUR DEPOSITS AND LEAKS

Every week, run the energy ledger.

- Deposits: Sleep, breath, movement, fuel, connection. What are you doing to build energy?
- Withdrawal leaks: Attention drains, people tax, system friction. What's bleeding you dry?
- Spends: Where are you investing energy with intention? Where are you wasting it?

If you're spending more than you're depositing, the system will fail. Period.

STEP 4: PROTECT YOUR PEAK WINDOWS

The week before your peak moment, your job is simple: Show up fresh. That means:

- Cutting low-value commitments
- Reducing travel if possible
- Sleeping like it's your job
- Running your reset loops religiously
- Protecting against people and environments that drain you

Aryna would play back-to-back tournaments leading up to a Slam, then show up exhausted. We had to build in rest windows, skip tournaments, and time her schedule so she peaked at the right moment. It felt counterintuitive, like she was doing *less*. But actually, she was doing *better*. Sustainable success isn't about doing more. It's about doing the right things at the right time.

BUILDING THE SYSTEM: A 90-DAY PROCESS

All right, you've got the frameworks. You've got the questions. Now, let's build the actual system. This isn't some hack or 7-day challenge. It's a 90-day process to install the Performance OS and make it permanent.

PHASE 1: AUDIT (DAYS 1-14)

Your first two weeks are about clarity.

WEEK 1: TRACK EVERYTHING

Carry a notebook. Every time you feel an energy shift—up or down—write it down.

- What were you doing?
- Who were you with?
- What had you just eaten, read, or experienced?

Don't judge or try to fix it yet. For now, just observe.

WEEK 2: IDENTIFY PATTERNS

Look at your notes. What patterns emerge?

- What consistently drains you?
- What consistently builds you?
- What environments elevate you? Which ones erode you?
- What relationships fuel you? Which ones bleed you?

Circle the top three leaks. Those are now your targets.

PHASE 2: BUILD (DAYS 15–45)

Now, you start building deposits and plugging leaks.

WEEK 3: INSTALL ONE TAKEOFF BLOCK

Pick your highest-leverage work. Schedule one 30-minute takeoff block. Turn off notifications. Close the door. Run the reset loop before you start: Roll your shoulders back, open your chest, breathe twice, set your posture, and aim at one clear task. Do this every day for seven days and track how it feels.

WEEK 4: ADD RECOVERY RITUALS

At the end of each day, run a descent ritual:

- Close any open loops.
- Write down tomorrow's first move.
- Spend five minutes reviewing: What worked well today? What needs work? What's the plan for tomorrow?

This will clear your mental cache, so you don't carry today's weight into tomorrow.

WEEK 5: PROTECT ONE BOUNDARY

Pick your biggest leak. Set one hard boundary to protect against it. Something like:

- No inbox checks after 7 PM.
- No meetings before 9 AM.
- Spend one day a week completely offline.
- Limit contact with one relationship.

Whatever it is, protect it as if your freedom depends on it.

WEEK 6: INTEGRATE BREATH AND MOVEMENT

Add one breathing drill before every high-stakes moment. Add one movement break every 90 minutes.

PHASE 3: SUSTAIN (DAYS 46–90)

The final six weeks are about making it permanent.

WEEKS 7–9: RUN THE FULL FLIGHT PLAN

Every day should include:

- One takeoff block (prime work)
- Two cruise blocks (steady work)
- One descent ritual (recovery)

Track your energy ledger weekly. Adjust as needed.

WEEKS 10–12: CHARACTER WORK

Each week, answer the Character Growth Assessment questions:

- Who do I need to become this week?
- What would future me do in this situation?
- What's the thing I'm avoiding that I need to face?

Write it down. Share it with someone you trust. Then, do the hard thing.

WEEK 13: REVIEW AND REFINE

At the end of 90 days, run a full audit:

- What works well?
- What needs work?
- What's the plan for the next 90 days?

The system isn't finished; it's never finished. But now it's running.

THE MIRROR IS NOT OPTIONAL

Previously, we talked about the temptation and allure of self-deception. But you absolutely can't build a system if you're deceiving yourself. You can have all the frameworks in the world. All the tools. All the routines. But if you're not honest with yourself about what's actually happening, none of it works.

I've watched it destroy careers, relationships, and teams. People who had everything—talent, resources, opportunity—couldn't look in the mirror long enough to admit where they were lying to themselves. Instead, they kept adding new apps, new hacks, and new programs. If you want this to work, radical honesty is nonnegotiable. It means answering questions like:

- Where are you avoiding truth in the name of progress?
- What's the cost of the story you're telling yourself right now?
- Where are you blaming instead of owning?

Stop what you're doing. Take a step back. Look at yourself. See what's objectively happening. This is uncomfortable work. And because of that, most people never do it. But growth comes from the uncomfortable, and honesty will allow you to see where and how you can grow.

THE SYSTEM IN ACTION

After Wimbledon, Aryna and I rebuilt her system from the ground up. We ran the Three Big Questions:

- *What works well?* Her intensity. Her competitive fire. Her ability to grind.
- *What needs work?* Her emotional regulation. Her energy management across the season. Her relationship with pressure environments.
- *What's the plan?* Breathing drills before, during, and after every match. Energy audits every week. Scheduled rest windows leading into the US Open.

We applied the Four Big Qualifiers:

- *Objective:* Run the reset loop twice between every point.
- *100% control:* She controlled her breath, her posture, her response.

- *Highly specific:* Roll the shoulders back, open the chest, breathe in through the nose, out through the mouth, reset posture, and aim at the next point.
- *Regardless of the outcome:* Whether she was winning or losing, the loop stayed the same.

We worked through her Character Growth Assessment:

- *Who does she need to become?* Someone who can regulate emotions in hostile environments.
- *What would future Aryna do?* She wouldn't spiral. She'd reset and trust her process.
- *What scares her most?* Letting people see her as mentally weak.

Then we built her peak performance timeline:

- We mapped her schedule backward from the US Open.
- We cut two tournaments to create recovery windows.
- We protected her takeoff blocks for training.
- We scheduled cruise blocks for sponsor obligations.
- We built in descent rituals every night.

By the time we got to New York, she was more than prepared; she was aligned. Her energy, emotions, and environment were all working together. And when she stepped into Arthur Ashe Stadium in the final, she wasn't a fighter brawling for a win. She was a warrior with focused intent. The pressure of that moment revealed her code for what it had become. She won in straight sets and defended her title, becoming the first woman since Serena Williams to go back-to-back at the US Open. That's what a system without cracks looks like. That's how an aligned Pressure Code runs.

YOUR TURN

Alright, you've got the blueprint. Now, it's time to build.

Start with the Three Big Questions:

1. What works well?
2. What needs work?
3. What's the plan?

Run your plan through the Four Big Qualifiers:

1. Is it extremely objective?
2. Do I have 100% control over it?
3. Is it highly specific?
4. Will I do this regardless of the outcome?

Answer the Character Growth Assessment:

1. Who do I need to become?
2. What would future me do?
3. What's the thing I'm avoiding that I need to face?

Map your peak performance timeline:

- Identify your peak moments.
- Build your energy rhythm (takeoff, cruise, descent).
- Audit your deposits and leaks.
- Protect your peak windows.

Then, commit to the 90-day process:

- Days 1–14: Audit
- Days 15–45: Build
- Days 46–90: Sustain

The system won't be perfect on day 1. It won't be easy. And there will be moments when you want to quit and go back to the old way of doing things. But that's what it takes for the person who got you here to become the person who keeps you here. With a tuned and aligned Performance OS, you can write your own legacy.

BUILDING TOWARD MASTERY

The rhythm of the loop is simple: know, adjust, apply, notice, repeat.

Elite performers fall apart when they skip the first step—when they try to fix without seeing or grind without recalibrating. The best I've coached don't add more tools; they tighten the loop. They notice faster, recover faster, and return to alignment faster.

That's the real engine behind progress—not intensity, but awareness practiced until it becomes reflex.

Chapter Eight

LONGEVITY AND LEGACY

After Aryna won the US Open in 2025, the press wanted to know how she did it. How she held her composure. How she defended her title when so many others couldn't. How she became the first woman since Serena Williams to go back-to-back in New York.

But I was thinking about a different question.

How do you *keep* doing it? Sure, winning once is an achievement. Often a spectacular one. But sustaining it? That's something else. And most people confuse the two. They think if they can just reach the goal—the promotion, the championship, the exit, the number on the scale—they'll have arrived. But arrival is a myth. The moment you stop moving forward with intention, you start sliding backward. Or said another way, life is in constant motion. If you stop and settle, stop paying attention, or assume you've "won," the universe will keep moving without you, which leaves you chasing your own tail (at best), inadequately prepared for the next cycle of obstacles and opportunities. As soon as you believe you've made it, the universe will remind you otherwise.

OBTAINING VERSUS SUSTAINING

I wrote this earlier, but it bears repeating: The person who got you here needs to become the person who keeps you here. That sentence sounds simple, but most people miss it entirely.

Early in Aryna's career, she'd win matches on sheer force, then collapse in the moments that mattered most: the Australian Open final against Keys, the French Open final against Gauff, Wimbledon semifinals. Over and over again, it was the same pattern.

Intensity burns out.

Effort has a ceiling.

Your code breaks under enough pressure.

Your goal in aligning your Performance OS is not to find new ways to grind harder but to actually become someone different. Someone whose system holds when pressure spikes. Someone who doesn't need to rely on adrenaline because their operating system runs cleanly.

YOUR CAPACITY RISES WHEN YOUR CHARACTER DEEPENS

Physics doesn't lie. Systems that only burn energy eventually break down. Grinding is acceleration without adaptation—it drains faster than it builds. But systems that convert energy instead of consuming it last longer. The same law applies to people. The ones who sustain success aren't powered by force; they're built by identity. A person who *obtains* success through grinding will eventually hit a wall. The person who *sustains* success has built an identity that carries the load.

I think about life like a phone battery. Every day, you've got a charge. You build energy, spend it, recover, repeat. That's the daily cycle. But underneath that, there's something more permanent—the battery itself. It's the actual material that holds the charge. You can have a fresh charge every morning and still burn out if the battery's capacity is shrinking.

The lifespan of your phone depends on how you treat it. Keep it in ideal conditions—don't drop it, don't leave it in the sun, don't overcharge it—and the battery lasts. Abuse it, and the capacity degrades. Eventually, even a full charge doesn't hold.

The same goes with people. If you're not managing your energy, your emotions, and your environment the right way, you're burning through your battery faster than you think. I know what that feels like. For years, I survived on almost no sleep. Not insomnia—this wasn't tossing and turning. I was lying in bed, knowing I wasn't dropping into deep sleep. No REM. No recovery. Sometimes I'd go two, even three days without sleeping at all. And somehow, I kept functioning. Kept working. Kept coaching.

But I was not okay.

I thought I was just built differently and that I could override the system. What I didn't realize was that the system was breaking down behind the scenes—silently, but violently. My blood markers were off the charts. My cardiovascular risk profile was so bad that one doctor told me I could literally drop dead at any moment. Organs were shutting down. Certain parts of my brain were going offline. And not a single person could figure out how I was still upright, let alone performing at the level I was.

Turns out, I had spent decades compensating. Polyphasic rest, breathwork, ground recovery, micro switch-offs throughout the day—before a lecture, in the car, between matches. I wasn't fixing the problem, but I was managing the consequences just enough to keep going.

Eventually, I found the right doctor. She connected the dots—trauma, PTSD-like responses to sleep, and even the biochemistry behind the shutdown. I had been powering through for years, but the Performance OS was burning out. All the things I was doing to help myself were speeding up the decline.

That's what most people don't see. They look at the tactics—the breathwork, the supplements, the mental toughness—and think that's what's keeping them high-performing. But the system underneath? If it's not sound, everything collapses eventually. It's not always dramatic; sometimes, it's invisible. You just erode—slowly, quietly—instead of falling off a cliff. Until one day, you look around and realize you're still functioning, but you're not really living. Your body's moving, but the lights are off inside.

That's how you end up walking around the last half of your life miserable: addicted to something, your relationships destroyed, and feeling burned out. You look in the mirror and don't like who you've become. And sadly, you don't even know how you got there.

Or worse—you hit what looks like an identity crisis. Because everything you were, everything people liked about you, was tied to what you did, not who you are. And when you can't do it anymore, there's nothing left.

That's the biggest risk I see with elite performers. The people around them like them because of what they accomplish, not who they are. And when the accomplishments stop, the relationships evaporate. Sustaining success means becoming someone people value for who you are, not just what you produce.

THE LOYAL FEW

Longevity starts with the people you keep close. The small circle of people who keep you honest, keep you on track, and show up for you in the way you need—even when you don't ask. With Aryna, it's me, Anton (her tennis coach), and a few others. The culture we've built isn't something we talk about much. We don't have to. It just exists. She doesn't wonder about our intentions. She doesn't question whether Anton and I are aligned. She doesn't worry about who's undermining whom. It's not even a thought, and that's the point.

Trust at that level doesn't happen by accident. It takes intention, clear roles, shared values, and loyalty. *Through loyalty, you gain trust. With trust comes freedom. To maintain that freedom, remain loyal.* That's what my sensei taught me years ago, and it's what holds together every high-performing team I've ever seen.

When someone on Aryna's team shows up anxious, I remove them from the room. Not because I'm controlling, but because their anxiety is contagious. She can't hear their words, but she can literally smell their state through chemosignals. Your body releases signals about your emotional state through sweat. Fear, stress, confidence—they all leak into the environment.[9] Her system absorbs it before she even knows why.

So, we protect her environment. We don't let noise in. We don't let doubt in. We keep the circle tight, and we keep it clean because the people around you either elevate you or erode you. They will put pressure on your code. There's no neutral. Believe me, I've been in rooms that could tank your nervous system the second you walked in.

One gym I worked with years ago had everything on paper—solid programs, big-name coaches, a decent client base. But the atmosphere? It was a mess. Staff would joke crudely across the weight floor, drop f-bombs in front of clients, and gossip loudly at the front desk. No one showed up early. No one stayed late. Everyone was in self-preservation mode. Not because they were bad people, but because there was no container, no structure, no standard. Just unchecked chaos passed off as "being real." That's what people miss about performance environments. Culture is enforced by what you tolerate.

I started with things like posture, energy, and tone. When I showed up, I didn't match the chaos. I grounded myself, slowed my speech, and cleaned up my interactions. I asked the right questions at the right time in the right tone. I narrowed my access, not out of arrogance, but stewardship. I started setting the tempo, not reacting to it.

Some people shifted fast. Others took time. A few even left, but that's how it goes. The system shifted. The space got quieter and more focused. The clients stayed longer, and the staff started self-regulating. I created a rhythm that their bodies could trust.

That's what leadership looks like when it's working. It's not about volume or control. It's just a clear signal, delivered consistently, until it becomes the norm, which is why I'm so ruthless about Aryna's environment. Because what seems like "just energy" is actually data. Her system reads everything. You can't afford to have volatility sitting courtside. It doesn't matter how skilled someone is—if their nervous system is unstable, it leaks into the air. And while elite performers don't always notice what's happening, their systems do. Their bodies start bracing, and they spiral.

So, we manage access. Not because we're gatekeeping egos, but because the climate matters more than the content. The wrong tone at the wrong time? It can derail a season.

If you're building a high-performing team, this has to become part of your operating system. You can't just curate résumés. You have to curate resonance. Who's aligned? Who sets the rhythm? Who shows up with clarity, even when things get loud?

Remember, it's not just who's on the team but what they're allowed to say and when. I learned this working with outside specialists—biomechanics experts, physios, agents, even media coaches. Everyone wants to help. But too often, that help becomes a flood.

When we brought in a biomechanics expert to support Aryna's serve, the guy had a mountain of knowledge and years of elite experience. He was brilliant technically, but also eager to prove his value, like most people are. And that meant a tendency to overload. With good intentions, he'd lay out everything he knew, dumping the full encyclopedia of knowledge when what Aryna really needed was a Post-it note.

That's where things fall apart. You don't need every fact about torque and shoulder load before stepping on the court. You need the right thing delivered in the right way, at the right time, by the right person.

So, Anton and I mapped it out. We asked: What do we actually need from this person? Not everything he could offer—just what would move Aryna forward. And once we knew that, we narrowed it down even further. Of all the elements of the serve he could address, which one or two mattered most? What would actually land? What would she trust? What would be receivable?

Because trust isn't automatic, the delivery matters. We controlled when that person traveled with us, what sessions they were part of, and what they were allowed to focus on. Sometimes, we even filtered the message through someone else entirely—Anton, a partner, even an agent. Sometimes, the messenger matters more than the message.

That's how I coach: protecting the system from noise. It's knowing your athlete, your people, your team. The job for me is to make the right signal land at the right moment, so it turns into action. And it's definitely not about showing off how much you know.

PEOPLE LIKE YOU FOR WHAT YOU DO OR WHO YOU ARE

One of the hardest questions elite performers face is this: Do people like you for what you do, or who you are? I've worked with ultra-high-net-worth individuals who can't trust anyone around them. They assume everyone wants something. And often, they're right. They've built their identity entirely on output: wealth, status, access, performance.

When that's your foundation, relationships become transactional. People stick around for what you provide, not who you are. And the moment you stop producing, they leave. That's why so many successful people feel isolated. They've spent years grinding to the top, but they've never built the character that sustains connection.

Aryna faced a version of this after Roland-Garros in 2025. The press was brutal. Fans questioned her composure. People started doubting whether she could win the big ones. And in that moment, she had a choice: Keep grinding the same way and hope it clicks, or face the thing she'd been avoiding.

ALIGNMENT BETWEEN WHO YOU ARE AND WHAT YOU DO

Sustainability lives at the intersection of who you are and what you do. Early in my career, I took roles that didn't align with my character. I knew they wouldn't last. There was friction everywhere—between what I valued and what the job demanded, between how I wanted to show up and what the environment required. Those roles burned me out fast. Not because I wasn't capable, but because there was no alignment. I was forcing intensity to cover the gap, and you can only do that for so long.

When I finally found work that aligned with who I am—coaching, mentoring, building systems that help people perform at their best—everything changed. The pressure didn't disappear, but it stopped feeling like a grind. Decision-making got easier because I wasn't fighting myself anymore.

Early in Aryna's career, she was trying to be someone she wasn't: calm, composed, the "right" kind of champion. But that wasn't her. She's a wildfire full of intensity, raw with a competitive edge. The breakthrough came when she stopped trying to suppress that and started learning how to harness it. The goal is not to program the code to kill the fighter. Rather, it's building a Pressure Code to channel the warrior.

It's the same fire, just a different system, which is what alignment looks like. You don't have to become someone else. You become the best version of who you already are.

NOT EVERY STEP UP IS FORWARD

There was this guy, Mike, one of my best sales guys back in the club days. He wasn't loud or slick. He just cared. He knew everyone's name, remembered who'd had knee surgery, who was training for their first 5k, etc. You could feel the shift when he walked in. He made the place feel alive.

After a few record months, the offers started coming in—management roles with bigger paychecks and titles that looked great on a résumé. He'd come find me every time with the same question: "Should I take it?"

We'd sit in my office, usually late, both tired and half-laughing at how serious it all felt. I'd have him walk through what he'd gain and what he'd lose. Then, I'd ask the only question that ever really mattered: "Can you still do what you love if you take it?"

He'd go quiet for a minute, lean back in the chair, stare at the ceiling. Then he'd shake his head. "Not really."

Mike knew himself. He knew his rhythm—on the floor, with people, in motion. He knew the second he traded that for meetings and memos he'd lose what made him great.

Most people don't have that kind of awareness. They see a promotion and stop asking questions. But Mike understood that not every step up is forward. He stayed where he could breathe. He kept building, and he kept people coming back. And years later, he still had the same energy and drive.

Sustainability isn't burnout disguised as ambition. It's not chasing titles that sound better than they feel. True sustainability is staying in rhythm with what actually makes you alive.

There's a kind of discipline in that—knowing when *not* to move. Most people equate growth with motion, but momentum without awareness is just drifting. Longevity is about coherence, but you can't sustain what doesn't fit your nature. You want your code designed so that all parts of you are telling the same story, and your body, mind, and emotions are moving in one rhythm instead of competing for control.

HOW TO SUSTAIN WITHOUT BURNING OUT

So how do you actually do this? How do you sustain success without destroying yourself in the process? It comes back to the same principles that run through every chapter of this book. But now, we're talking about applying them long term. Not for one match, not for one quarter—for years.

SUSTAINING ENERGY

If you want longevity, treat energy like the finite resource it is. One of the most underused energy tools? Novelty. It's not bio hacks and sleep optimization—but joy, play. The kind of mental and physical movement that wakes you up instead of wears you down.

There's real research behind it—on how novelty supports emotional regulation, mental health, and system recharge. Psychologists call it *psychological richness*—the way fresh experiences and new challenges energize your system instead of draining it.[10] But you don't need a lab study to feel it. You've lived it. A new activity, a lighthearted competition, a challenge that's fun instead of forced. These things expand your capacity. They stretch your battery.

Nor do you need an expansive team or complex program to make it happen. One of my clients started setting five-minute timers to race himself through boring tasks. Another built mini-challenges into his recovery days—trying to beat his step count or hold a plank longer just for fun. That might sound off, but it works. It taps into something that grinding can't. Over time, this becomes one of the most powerful levers for sustaining performance.

SUSTAINING EMOTIONS

Regulation beats motivation every time. Motivation fades, but regulation holds. Aryna used to spiral when things went wrong, her frustration bleeding everywhere. Now, she runs the reset loop—roll, breathe, set, aim—twice between every point.

That loop isn't about judging the last point but intentionally returning to the present. That's one of the most misunderstood parts of elite performance. People confuse self-awareness with self-evaluation. They're not the same. Self-awareness is tuning into your body, your breath, your state. It's recognizing when you're tense, when you're clear, and how the environment is affecting you. Self-evaluation is judging. It's asking, "How am I doing?" in the middle of doing it—which is exactly what kills flow.

If you want to perform, you train awareness. You quiet the scoreboard in your head and anchor to the moment. Evaluation has its place, but only after the fact. That's when you run your post-match debrief: What worked? What didn't? What's the plan? But during—there's only presence, awareness.

If you want longevity, train emotional regulation like a skill.

I learned that one early—way before I knew the term for it. Back when I was a kid, I'd disappear into the library whenever I could. Home was unpredictable and chaotic, as I've shared. And outside? Worse. Sometimes, I had people following me, harassing me. One massive guy, strung out on drugs, started stalking me on the buses. He chased me down the street once, smashing his fists against the window.

So, I had to hide.

Not just inside the library, but just to get there. I'd sneak through wooded areas and back alleys, always watching the cars, timing my sprint to the door so no one would see where I was going. I had to stay invisible.

Once I got inside, the world went quiet, and I could relax for a time. I read books about cars and space and martial arts, manuals about how things worked, fit together, and held up under pressure. A lot of that was because of my dad. He was a mechanic, and I used to watch him work on motorcycles, learning the parts. Those library books became my anchors. They reminded me there was an order to things, even when everything around me felt out of control.

I'd also read about samurai and ninjas. Not just the cool, flashy stuff, but their code. Their discipline. Their energy. Their environment. There was a vocabulary out there for what I was chasing, and I was just starting to learn it. That, and a better system to survive. Sometimes, that included candy—that I stole. I'd buy one box of Good & Plenty, stash it outside, go back in with the receipt, and grab a second one to stretch it out. That was my food for the day. I'd sit in the library for hours, sipping from the water fountain and eating a couple of pieces at a time. Sugar and structure.

That was the beginning of my operating system: regulating fear, managing energy, creating safety through precision. That's the muscle I built before I ever learned to coach. That was the Pressure Code in the early days of the refiner's fire.

SUSTAINING ENVIRONMENT

This may land as a hard truth: You can't sustain performance in a toxic environment. It doesn't matter how tough you are. The right people, the right spaces, the right cues—they either lift you or drain you. Aryna's "hate relationship" with Wimbledon showed what happens when the environment works against you. Her US Open title showed what happens when it works for you.

If you want longevity, you have to shape your environment with the same care you give your training. They're one system, and when they align, sustainable performance stops being a dream and starts being your default. That's because what's around you determines what comes out of you. And most people are leaking energy from things they don't even notice—lighting, posture, layout, conversations they keep having but shouldn't be, people they should've cut loose a year ago but didn't. The physical environment sets a baseline for emotional tone, and emotional tone sets your access to energy.

In my gym-running days, I saw that pattern everywhere. There were those who trained hard and showed up consistently, but something always felt off. They weren't evolving. And it wasn't about effort—it was the room. It was too sterile, too tight, or too packed with the wrong people. The energy never lifted.

So, we brought in music that changed the athletes' posture. We made warm-ups more reactive. We added mini competitions that forced people to move, interact, and respond. The shift was immediate. People left sessions more energized than when they came in. And *that's* the sign you're doing it right. The pressure from training isn't supposed to drain your life force—it's supposed to create lift.

That principle scaled. Whether I'm working with a tennis pro or a founder or a CFO, I look for friction in their environments. You don't need more motivation. You just need fewer distractions and leaky inputs and cleaner emotional air. You want to go deep? You need stillness in the room and clarity about who's allowed in.

As I wrote earlier, your environment is never neutral: It's either building you or breaking you. To make it sustainable over the long term, there's a martial arts principle that applies. *Ma-ai* is the art of managing the distance between you and whatever you're facing. Too close, and you lose perspective. Too far, and you lose control. People spend years standing too close to what's wrong for them and too far from what they really want. They tell themselves they can adapt, endure, and grind it out. But that will slowly erode you.

The right distance gives you power. And sometimes that right distance means leaving one environment for another. I watched that play out with a young woman named Ruby. She was one of my salespeople at a luxury gym I was managing. She was sharp, ambitious, and quick with people. She could close deals and light up a room. But there was something in her eyes that didn't match her performance—like she was running out of air in a space that looked glamorous from the outside but was suffocating her on the inside.

Outside of work, she was chasing something else: modeling, acting, building a life that was creative and free. She had the hunger, the work ethic, and the edge. But within that sales environment, her energy was leaking out through the cracks. She'd show up drained, second-guessing herself, smiling through exhaustion. One afternoon after another long week, I pulled her aside. She was frustrated—talking about schedules, team politics, the usual noise. But underneath all that was fear. I could feel it. So, I told her straight: "You've got to go."

She blinked at me like she'd misheard.

I was her boss, and she expected a pep talk, not a release. But I could see the truth as clear as a bad stance in sparring. If she stayed, she'd calcify. She'd lose the rhythm that made her special. I told her, "You're standing in the wrong place for the life you're trying to build."

That's *ma-ai*. The understanding that, based on where you are in relation to the obstacle or fight, your actions need to be in alignment with the desired outcome. That includes controlling the distance:

when to enter, when to pivot, when to sidestep, when to fully commit, when to close the distance . . . and when to exit.

Ruby hesitated. She was scared and uncertain, but eventually she took my advice. She didn't just leave the job. She left the noise, the misalignment, the environment that had her shrinking instead of expanding.

Ruby went on to model, host, and act on MTV, in high-profile campaigns, even playing a role in a John Wick movie. She became a global name. And no, I'm not saying I made that happen. She did. But I saw what most people miss: She had the skill; she just needed the right environment for it to breathe.

That moment changed something in me too. It reminded me that leadership isn't about keeping people—it's about knowing when to let them go. Sometimes the right move for longevity isn't to fix an environment. It's showing the way to the exit.

That's one of the hardest truths for elite performers to accept. We confuse discipline with endurance. We think staying in a situation that drains us is noble. It's not. It's just fear dressed up as loyalty. Martial arts taught me that awareness without courage is paralysis. You can know your stance is off, you can feel your balance slipping. But until you move, nothing changes.

That's what Ruby did. She moved with *tomaranu kokoro*—an indomitable spirit. That's true bravery: the willingness to act on what awareness reveals. Even when it means walking out of the room and leaving the current environment behind.

Chapter Nine

THE ROOM DECIDES

I've spent more time than I can count in gyms around the world. Tokyo, Buenos Aires, Munich, Melbourne—you name it. Walk in, and you can usually tell everything you need to know within a few seconds. The air, the posture, the noise (or lack of it), the vibe all tell you. The energy in a room is never random; it's either engineered for success or it's eroding.

Once, I walked into one such gym and didn't need to see a single rep. I could already feel it. Nobody was talking. Nobody was connecting. The energy was flat, disconnected, and performative. One guy was doing wrist rolls in the corner, eyes glazed. Another was fake-hyping a teammate with a dead tone—trying to sound engaged, but his nervous system wasn't buying it. Nobody made eye contact.

The coach cracked a joke, but it died midair. And when the sparring started, it wasn't explosive. It was frantic, sloppy. They were competing, but nobody was performing. That's how I knew the culture was toxic. And I don't mean toxic in the headline-grabbing way—no screaming or throwing weights. It was a quiet toxic. The kind that happens when trust is low, but no one wants to say it. When leadership is performative, and people mistake surface-level hype for deep alignment. When everyone says they want to win, but no one's willing to hold each other accountable for how they show up.

Culture always tells the truth. And the room always decides.

So I asked the coach a question: "Do you want these guys to compete, or do you want them to connect?" Okay, trick question, because the answer is "Both."

Competition without connection breeds distrust. Connection without competition breeds comfort. Everyone is good at looking like they're busy, but that's not the same as being challenged. And you can't achieve both without culture. Culture isn't values painted on a wall. It's the embodied rules of the room—what's tolerated, what's reinforced, and what's sacred.

THE CULTURE AUDIT: WHAT I SEE IN THE FIRST THREE MINUTES

You don't need a full team meeting to diagnose a culture. You need about three minutes. When I walk into a room, I scan five things that tell me almost everything I need to know:

- Posture
- Pace
- Eye contact
- Language
- Micro-recoveries

Each one is subtle, but together, they reveal the underlying code of the room.

POSTURE

Posture is emotional geometry. You can see it before anyone says a word. Is someone rooted, or are they bracing? Are their shoulders lifted from tension or dropped into readiness? Do they take up space with calm authority or shrink behind performative energy?

In high-trust rooms, posture reflects ownership. In low-trust rooms, it reflects protection. I watch for slumped chests, twitchy micro-movements, arms crossed just a little too long. People call it body language, but it's really nervous system language. It's your physiology voting on whether it feels safe enough to show up or whether it's already halfway into retreat. When someone's standing present, they're telling the room: *I'm here, and I'm not performing for you—I'm aligned with something deeper.* When they're posturing, the body says something different: *I'm not okay, but I don't trust this room enough to say it.*

In elite performance, posture becomes an x-ray of belief. It not only signals readiness but shapes it. There's a popular idea that holding a "power pose" can shift your hormonal state—testosterone up, cortisol down. But that research has never been replicated. What does hold up is simpler: How you carry yourself changes how you feel, and how others respond to you. Posture is both a psychological and social signal. Your body teaches your brain what's happening, and the room reads it before you say a word. It's a way to reconnect to what's already in you—your groundedness, your strength, your clarity—and let your body broadcast it before your mouth ever opens.

In coaching, I often say: "You can't bullshit your nervous system." Posture is one of the fastest ways to feel the room's truth. You'll see it everywhere. In the guy who puffs up his chest but keeps backing up. In the athlete who stands tall until the coach walks by. In the team meeting where everyone's posture collapses the moment the leader speaks.

When posture matches intention, people move more cleanly, make decisions more quickly, and recover more efficiently. By training your energy, emotions, and environment to work together in real time, you create the internal and external alignment that allows strength to show up.

PACE

This one often gets overlooked. In frantic rooms, people rush from one thing to the next. There's no breath between transitions, no reset between reps. It's anxiety versus urgency, and there's a difference between a high tempo and an unregulated nervous system. You can feel it. People are skipping steps. Voices are too loud. Movements are sharp, not precise. The body is moving, but the mind isn't leading.

In well-run rooms, you'll find cadence and deliberate motion. You see it in the transitions as much as in the training. The space between matters. Great teams know when to step in, when to pause, and when to recalibrate. It's about hitting the right rhythm for the task, the person, the moment.

As I like to say, rhythm matters more than speed.

So when I walk into a room, I'm not just watching what people are doing—I'm watching *how* they move. Are they rushed? Are they rattled? Are they syncing with each other or running their own private scripts? And I don't just mean on the surface. I'm watching the breath, the micro-pauses, the way someone carries their nervous system.

Elite performance is about knowing when to push and when to pull back. It's about rhythm and recovery because recovery is an essential part of the work, not just something that happens after. Most people treat recovery like a reward, something you earn after you grind. The best performers build it into the rhythm, between reps, matches, conversations, quarters, or campaigns.

They recover on purpose.

I teach athletes to reset between points, not at the end of the match. I coach executives to pause between meetings, not at the end of the week. If you wait for the full stop, you've already missed the signs. And eventually, your code folds under the pressure. That's what happened with Aryna early on. She trained relentlessly but never reset. Her rituals were thin. Her off-court rhythm didn't support her on-court performance. She thought taking a break meant losing her edge. But that edge was blunted every time she ignored recovery.

Now? Two breath cycles between every point. A physical cue to drop the last rally. A refocus cue before the next one. Exhaling on purpose. It's not dramatic. It's not sexy. But it's a system. Zooming out, even for a beat, so you can zoom back in with clarity.

That's what rhythm recovery looks like.

Remember, urgency without rhythm burns people out. And rhythm without urgency puts them to sleep.

EYE CONTACT

First, look at who avoids it. Then, look at who dominates it. You'll see the power dynamics immediately. In fragile systems, eye contact becomes a threat cue. People either flinch away from it or overcompensate—using it as a dominance display rather than a connection point. And the nervous system picks up on it before the mind does.[11] If the eyes are darting, glazed, or hyper-fixed, it's a readout on the room's safety settings. And you can't fake safety, nor can you coach trust into a group that's leaking it through their gaze.

In high-trust rooms, eye contact is fluid. People check in with each other naturally. Eyes meet, then drift. They don't stare through each other like competitors in a standoff. They don't glance away like they're hiding something. There's presence without posturing. Awareness without aggression.

This matters because the eyes are more than a social tool—they're a biological signal. From an evolutionary standpoint, sustained eye contact was a survival risk. It meant challenge and conflict. In modern rooms, those same instincts apply. The difference is that in high-performing teams, eye contact becomes a reassurance signal—a way of saying: *I'm here. I see you. We're good.*

Here's what I tell athletes: Don't just scan the room. *Feel it* through the eyes. Are you seeing people who are with each other, or are you seeing people who are watching each other?

And leaders? You set the tone. If you're avoiding eye contact—if you're disconnected, scattered, looking at your phone instead of your people—they feel it. Trust erodes in those silent moments. You just have to be present rather than intense.

Fragile rooms stare past each other. Strong rooms see each other.

LANGUAGE

Language is the most honest indicator of leadership. If you want to know what a team really believes, listen to how they speak when the tension is high and things go sideways. That's when language reveals everything.

In high-trust cultures, language is clear, direct, and clean. Instructions are delivered without hesitation and with ownership. Corrections land without ego. There's no showboating or sugarcoating. Just clarity and care.

In low-trust cultures, the language gets murky. They provide vague feedback with passive phrasing that only offers hints instead of the truth. You hear more disclaimers than direction: "I don't want to step on toes, but—" or "This might be off, but maybe try . . ." That fear kills performance.

You can also hear the team's identity in their language: "We get to do this," not "We have to." "We own it," not "We'll see." Listen for phrases that reveal agency or the lack of it. Teams can easily talk their way into dysfunction.

The tone matters too. When stress hits, leaders either stabilize or spike the energy level. A fast, frantic tone ramps up tension. A slow, certain tone calms the system. Most people don't realize they're doing it—but the nervous system of the room knows.

And here's the deeper cut: Language doesn't just reflect state—it shapes it. Say "I'm overwhelmed," and cortisol goes up. Say "I'm in control," and your brain starts aligning with it.[12]

So if you want to understand a team's culture, don't just look at the results. *Listen* to the words used, the way people give feedback, their self-talk, and how they respond to failure. If you hear blame, vagueness, or self-doubt, there's rot in the system. If you hear ownership, specificity, and clarity, you're in a room that knows how to lead itself.

MICRO-RECOVERIES

This might be the most important element of a culture audit. When something breaks—a mistake, a missed cue, a dropped ball—how fast does the team reset? Do they blame? Do they freeze? Or do they breathe, recenter, and move forward? Recovery is more than just the physical. When done right, it becomes an essential part of your culture. The best rooms train micro-resets into the rhythm of everything they do.

I was taught in martial arts that recovery isn't what happens after the fight. It's what happens during the fight. You get clipped, you stumble, or you miss your mark—what you do in the next second determines everything. Freeze, and you get hit again. Panic, and your technique falls apart. But if you can reset—just enough to recenter your breath, feel your stance, square your eyes—you're still in it. You haven't lost the fight until you stop recovering.

That's what recovery looks like in performance. It's not a dramatic comeback or a motivational swell of energy. Recovery is just micro-adjustments that keep you from spiraling. One breath. One cue. One choice.

In high-performance rooms, you don't wait until something breaks to practice this. You build recovery into the rhythm. You normalize micro-resets. You train the team to recover together because that stabilizes the system. It keeps energy from leaking, and emotions from cascading. It turns failure into feedback.

When someone blows a rep, drops a ball, or fumbles a cue, it's not the mistake that matters. It's what happens next. Is there blame? Is there hesitation? Or does the system absorb it and recenter?

Micro-recovery is the difference between performers and professionals. Performers rely on adrenaline to carry them through. Pros train to expect disruption, and they don't personalize it. They reset quickly, quietly, and without drama. And they do it so consistently that it becomes cultural.

Recovery isn't just an individual trait. It's a team trait. A nervous system trait. A sign that the room is safe enough to fail and sturdy enough to rebound. In rooms like that, you'll notice the pace stays consistent. The eyes stay forward. The breath stays steady. Mistakes don't get ignored, but they don't hijack the room either.

In the wrong culture, a mistake is the beginning of the spiral. In the right culture, it's another rep in the rhythm of progress.

These five cues don't take long to spot. But they reveal whether a culture is reactive or regulated. Whether it runs on fear, hype, or trust. Whether performance is held together by adrenaline or by something deeper—what I call cultural coherence. When people know what's expected, and they trust the system around them, everything flows more smoothly. But when people start protecting their corners, deferring to leaders, or quietly tolerating dysfunction, performance erodes—whether anyone says it out loud or not.

That's why the room decides. Always.

REWRITING THE ROOM

Reading the room is only half the skill. The real test is knowing how to rewrite it. It's one thing to walk into a broken culture and name what's off. Anyone can play culture cop. The hard part is knowing how to shift it without preaching, without forcing, and without pretending that values printed on a wall are the same thing as values held in the body.

Because let's be honest: Most people already know what's wrong. They just don't know how to interrupt it without making things worse. In high-performance environments, culture doesn't change through speeches but through signals: tiny, precise inputs that tell the nervous system it's okay to show up differently here. Not safer in theory, but safer in practice. And the people who know how to send those signals? They're the ones who rewrite the room.

I've watched it happen dozens of times.

THE NERVOUS SYSTEM OF THE ROOM

Culture lives in the nervous system. You don't fix a reactive culture by telling people to "be more open." You fix it by showing them—through breath, through eye contact, and through presence—that openness isn't a risk, that disagreement won't get punished, that feedback won't get weaponized, and the room can hold discomfort without collapsing.

That's where the culture shifts.

It's in the moment someone fumbles a pass and looks up, waiting to see if they'll get chewed out—or supported. It's in the moment a junior team member challenges a call, and everyone waits to see if the room holds or tightens. It's in the leader who doesn't flinch, doesn't deflect, doesn't posture—just says, "You're right. Let's adjust."

Every moment like that is a nervous system input. And when you stack enough of them, the room starts to change.

HOW TO REWIRE THE ROOM

Here's what I teach leaders, coaches, and teammates who want to change a room without becoming a motivational speaker.

LEAD WITH YOUR REGULATION

Your nervous system is contagious. If you're rushed, scattered, or reactive, the room will mirror it. If you're anchored, the room will ground itself faster. Before you speak, check your breath. Before you lead, clear your signal. Be the tone you want to set.

NAME WHAT'S TRUE—BUT WITHOUT DRAMA

Call out the tension, the leak, the disconnection—but do it cleanly. Don't blame. Don't moralize. Just say what you see: "We're scattered right now." "Feels like we're rushing." "Let's bring it back." Those simple, clear statements anchor the room.

INSTALL MICRO-REPS

Every team, every room, needs a rhythm, a reset cue, a shared anchor. For some, it's a breath before every rep. For others, a short check-in before every meeting. Whatever it is, make it repeatable. Recovery needs practice, not permission.

REINFORCE WHAT'S WORKING

When someone resets instead of reacting, name it. When someone speaks clearly instead of vaguely, reinforce it. Not in a cheerleading way, but with a grounded, quiet nod. People will follow what's reinforced.

PROTECT THE CONTAINER

If someone consistently brings chaos, leaks tension, or erodes trust, address it with clarity: "We're building something here. If you want to be part of it, we need alignment." Most teams don't fail from one explosion. They fail from death by a thousand tolerated micro-fractures.

THE VIBE MANAGER

Every room has its own rhythm, and every rhythm has its regulators. Sometimes it's the coach. Sometimes it's the captain. But more often, it's someone you'd never guess. The quiet one who notices when the room is tipping. The teammate who sees the breath tighten, the shoulders rise, the eyes flick away. They feel the moment before the moment breaks—and they adjust.

In elite environments, this role becomes sacred. I've come to think of it as the vibe manager—the person who doesn't just read the room but quietly rewrites it in real time. They're not the loudest voice. They're not the most decorated. But they're the ones who stabilize the system when it wobbles.

I saw it on Aryna's team after she won the US Open. Our tennis coach, Anton, wasn't just running drills. He was running the current. He'd clock when energy was getting too sharp or too loose. He'd crack a joke to break the tension, offer silence when words would only cloud the moment. The vibe managers don't tell people how to feel. They show the room that it's safe to feel differently, to reset, to take a breath. And that signal? It spreads faster than any directive. Most people miss the power of this role because it doesn't show up on stat sheets. You can't track it in metrics. But without it, cultures crumble. And with it, systems hold.

I've worked with all types of teams—tech teams, professional athletes, special forces units—and the highest-performing ones all had a person like this. Someone who could tune the frequency of the room without drawing attention to themselves. Someone who instinctively knew: We're drifting. Let's bring it back.

If you're reading this and thinking, *That's not me—I'm not in charge*, that's the point. You don't need a title to lead this way. You just need awareness, signal clarity, and the courage to model the tone you want the room to take on.

The best vibe managers don't wait for permission. They don't need credit. They don't even need to be right. They just stay clean. Steady. Tuned. And when the room hits static, they help restore coherence. Every system needs that person. The question is—are you willing to be that person?

LEADERSHIP IS CULTURAL ENGINEERING

You don't need to be the boss to shift a culture. You just need to take ownership of your presence.

A teammate can do it with a breath.

A coach can do it with a tone.

You emit more culture than you'll ever engineer. Moment by moment in how you move, how you speak, how you recover, and how you trust.

Charlene was the person in the room who taught me that. She wasn't a fighter, a sensei, or an elite performer, but she taught me one of the hardest lessons I've ever learned. Trust others, yes, but more importantly, trust yourself. She had this way of being fully open—no agenda, no judgment, no expectations. Just presence. And that kind of openness can be terrifying when you're not used to it. For me, it was. I'd built my life on control and composure. Charlene's openness felt like standing in sunlight after years of living underground.

She helped me see that I'd been living by my values all along—loyalty, purpose, passion, and trust—even when I didn't believe it. Her presence gave me permission to stop trying to prove those things and start embodying them, and that shifted everything. It changed how I coach, how I parent, how I love. It's the difference between showing up to fix people and showing up to stand beside them. Charlene didn't teach me technique; she reminded me who I already was. She set the culture in the room, making it safe for me to learn and grow.

That's what real coaches do.

Yes, the room always decides, but you can teach the room *what* that is.

THE DOJO

Wedged between a pawnshop and an adult bookstore was the dojo of my youth. It smelled like sweat and old vinyl, with mats worn so thin in spots you could feel the concrete beneath. But the energy in that room was real. Clean. Focused. Nobody talked about culture, but it was in everything. The way we bowed in. The way we showed up. The way no one faked it—because if you did, you got found out fast.

I was in that room as a 16-year-old when I took a hard shot to the ribs. Not a knockout, not even a point, but it caught me just right. It sent a jolt through my system—not pain, but panic. I froze. My body was still in the fight, but my mind had stepped out. I glanced at the edge of the mat, looking for approval, or maybe permission to collapse. That's when my sensei's voice cut through it, calm and exact.

"Reset."

I didn't know what he meant. I thought he was telling me to square up. But later, I realized he was telling me to come back. To re-enter. Not just the match—but myself. It wasn't about the mistake. It was about the moment after the mistake, when the real fight happens. You either stay present, or you get pulled out by the noise in your head.

How you navigate the room is a function of your operating system. It's the difference between teams that run hot and burn out and teams that stay sharp under pressure because they've trained to bounce back.

In that dojo, we didn't talk about emotional intelligence or nervous system regulation. We certainly didn't talk about a Pressure Code. But it was baked into everything. A missed block didn't trigger shame—it triggered a reset. You didn't apologize. You didn't collapse. You found your stance. You took your breath. You looked your opponent in the eyes and rejoined the rhythm of the fight.

That's what the best rooms do. They are not only part of the system and give it context, but they bring it to life.

FALSE CULTURE SIGNALS

Culture gets faked more than performance ever does. I've been in rooms that look elite on the outside, but the moment you breathe it in, you know it's just theater. The posture's performative. The language's rehearsed. The vibe's manicured, not lived.

That's the danger when you start mistaking signals for substance. I've coached inside billion-dollar companies where every hallway had a banner about integrity, but in the boardroom, you couldn't get a straight answer if your life depended on it. Culture isn't what's printed. It's what's practiced. And the moment you start confusing aesthetics for alignment, you lose the plot.

HYPE CAN LOOK LIKE ENERGY

Just because a room is loud doesn't mean it's alive. Sometimes, the volume's there to mask the fear underneath. The pacing, the clapping, the "Let's go"—they're not wrong. But if the tone is desperate instead of grounded, you're bleeding energy.

SILENCE CAN LOOK LIKE ALIGNMENT

I've been in meetings where no one pushed back, no one questioned a decision, and everyone nodded along. The leader walked out thinking, *We're solid*. What they didn't realize is that the whole team had just checked out emotionally. They weren't aligned—they were shutting down.

FEAR CAN LOOK LIKE DISCIPLINE

Just because people are tight, on time, and compliant doesn't mean they're bought in. I've seen athletes follow every protocol to the letter—but do it with clenched jaws, guarded eyes, and zero trust. That's not culture. That's control.

The above are all false positives. And if you're not careful, they'll trick you into thinking your system is working—right up until it collapses.

So how do you tell the difference?

Turn down the volume. Strip out the hype. Remove the coach. Pull back the external pressure. What you're left with—that's the real signal. If the room breathes better without you in it, you've built something real. If it collapses the moment you stop performing leadership, all you've built is dependency.

FIRST IN, LAST OUT

People ask me all the time how I got here. Coaches, trainers, people at events who want to do what I do. They want the secret.

There isn't one. But there is a principle: I made sure I was in the room.

Not metaphorically. Literally. Whatever room held the people I needed to learn from, the environments where the work was happening—I found a way to be there. Whether I was a fly on the wall or directly involved. Whether I got paid or had to volunteer. Didn't matter how I felt. Didn't matter how hard it was to get there. Didn't matter what it cost me. I just made sure I was where I needed to be.

Early on, I worked every event I could find. Marathons. Charity runs. Youth soccer. University training rooms. I got certified as a massage/sports therapist, then a first responder, then an athletic trainer—not to collect credentials, but because each one was a key to another door. And I just said yes. Anything that put me in the right environment, around the right people, doing the right things—yes.

When I showed up, I showed up first. Before anyone was setting up. I'd walk in while people were still unloading equipment and say, "Let me help." Then I stayed until the place was empty. First one there, last one out. Every single time. I worked my ass off, and I just made sure I was building trust and connection with people.

I wasn't networking in that cheesy, annoying way where you're trying to get something from everyone. I wasn't extracting. I was giving. That was really what I was thinking: *What can I give?* I wanted to give and learn and do the best I could.

Whoever they put me with, I was 100,000% with that person in that moment. No matter what. If they had me work with the most useless person there that nobody liked, I treated them like the most important person in the room. If they gave me the worst job, I was the best at it. That was my mindset. No matter what I was doing, I made sure I was the best at it.

People feel that. They know when you're there to take versus when you're there to serve.

I'd be helping out at a kids' soccer game, and a parent would walk up. Turns out they're the head athletic trainer at some organization. "Hey, what do you do? How'd you learn this? We've got an event coming up—you interested in helping out?"

Yes. Always yes.

I just knew—gut level—that if I kept showing up in the right places, around the right people, doing the right things to the best of my ability, good things would come around. I knew that if I stayed genuine, operated from my values, and kept placing myself in those environments, something would happen. And it did.

TREAT EVERY ROOM LIKE IT'S *THE* ROOM

One of my early teachers taught me this lesson before I even understood it.

This guy started the first airport massage kiosk—maybe the first in the country. By the time I met him, he was successful. Wealthy. But his story started somewhere else entirely.

He was homeless and living out of his car. Duct tape on the windows. Surviving on Top Ramen and water for weeks at a time. He had nothing except his hands and his willingness to show up.

He worked every event he could find—marathons, charity runs, whatever. And whoever sat in his chair got everything he had. He didn't know who they were. Didn't assume anything. He just did the work.

One day, a man sat down. My teacher treated him like everyone else—full presence, full care. They really connected—and it turned out he was an executive at Boeing.

A few weeks later, my teacher got a call. Boeing was looking to hire someone to treat their executive team. Would he be interested in coming in, giving a proposal?

Remember, he had no money, no physical therapy degree, and no connections. He was just some random massage guy living out of his car.

So of course he said yes. He scraped together everything he had and sold what he could live without. He borrowed money and starved himself for weeks so he could afford a suit.

When the day came, he showed up early—polished, prepared, professional. And the competition? Physical therapy groups with degrees and credentials. They strolled in late, wearing khakis or other casual clothes. Kind of cocky about it, too, like, *We're smarter. We have more knowledge. We're obviously going to win.*

Boeing chose the homeless guy who showed up early and was wearing a suit. That one opportunity became the foundation of everything and started him down the path that led to massive expansion and a chain of airport kiosks. And millions of dollars. And it started because he showed up at some random local run, gave everything he had to whoever was in front of him, and treated an unknown stranger like the most important person in the room.

You don't know who's showing up. You have no idea who's in front of you. You don't assume anything.

That story rewired something in me. It confirmed what I already felt in my gut: You never know which room holds the moment that changes everything.

So you show up to every room like it's that room. You give everything to every person like they're that person. You don't wait until you know who's important. You treat everyone like they are.

That's presence. That's what it means to be the room instead of just being in it.

Which brings me back to you.

CLOSING CHALLENGE: ARE YOU THE ROOM?

By now, you should be convinced: The room always decides.

The question is—are *you* the room? What I mean by that is, you're never passive or a passenger mentally. You're a part of the room by being the room itself. What you bring creates the room and defines what you have control of.

You've spent this chapter learning how to read a space—how posture, pace, tone, and attention shape everything that happens inside it. You've seen how energy leaks, how chaos spreads, how clarity feels when it lands. But at some point, observation has to turn into ownership.

Every environment you walk into is a reflection of your internal state. The air thickens when you're tense. It sharpens when you're clear. You can talk about strategy, culture, or communication all day—but underneath it all, people are reading you. When you walk into a gym, a boardroom, or your own home, the atmosphere shifts before you say a word. It's not magic; it's chemistry. We sense coherence and incoherence the same way we sense threats. The body knows first.[13]

So, if the room feels scattered, check your focus.

If the room feels cold, check your energy.

If the room feels anxious, check your breath.

This is where the practice of *zanshin*—awareness that extends beyond the self—begins. You see everything, even the space between things.

And this is where *mushin*—no thought, no noise, just pure presence—takes over.

The room doesn't just need your energy. It needs your steadiness, and it needs someone whose presence reminds everyone else to breathe.

Before you walk into your next meeting, match, or moment, pause:

Take one breath.

Let your shoulders roll back.

Feel the ground.

Don't ask, "What's the vibe here?" Instead, ask, "What am I broadcasting?" Your job isn't to hold the culture up. It's to install it deep enough that it holds without you, and that only happens when the culture is baked into the nervous system—not the slogans, not the optics, not the post-game soundbites.

The culture is in how the team communicates under pressure. It's in who speaks up when it's risky. It's in the way feedback lands—and whether it gets used or ignored. It's in the eyes. The tone. The body. The breath. Culture is embedded in your operating system, and if it's not running deep, it's just another app on the home screen—one that crashes when you need it most.

Conclusion

This book has been about something much simpler and harder than success alone. Your Pressure Code is about building a system that can hold the weight of your own potential. Every story, from the dojo to the tour, from Aryna to Charlene, from the health clubs to the quiet moments between flights, has pointed to the same truth. When the pressure hits, you don't rise to the level of your ambition; you fall back on the strength of your system.

We began with energy—learning that output is overrated if it isn't regulated. You saw what happens when the body is wired for survival, but the world demands flow. You learned that mastery isn't about adding more hours or effort; it's about managing the charge, about knowing when to hold and when to release. You learned that breath can reset a system faster than willpower ever could.

Then we moved through emotion—the place where awareness becomes empathy, and empathy becomes trust. It's the current that connects everything you do. Without it, performance is sterile. With it, it's alive.

Finally, we went deep into the environment—how every space

you walk into, from a gym to a boardroom to your own home, mirrors your internal state. You learned to read it before you tried to change it. To sense the air in the room before you spoke. To shift that air through your presence, not your volume.

These aren't stages you graduate from but frequencies you tune together. When energy, emotions, and environment align, the noise drops. Clarity returns. Performance stops being something you chase; it becomes the natural side effect of congruence.

That's the system I call the Pressure Code—not a set of hacks or habits, but a way of being. It's how your Performance OS responds under pressure, and how you move through the world when awareness, action, and alignment finally stop fighting each other. Like Aryna, finding composure beneath the glare of a global spotlight. Like Charlene, choosing openness instead of armor. Like Mike, stepping back from promotions to find peace. Like Ruby, walking out of the wrong room to find her rhythm again. Different stories, same lesson: Coherence beats control every time.

When you understand that principle, the work changes. You stop trying to be better and start trying to be honest. You begin to notice when your environment no longer fits. You listen when your body whispers that something's off. You stop outsourcing meaning to other people's approval and start earning your own peace. Because that's the real threshold of performance—when you no longer need chaos to prove you're alive.

You've spent this book walking through other people's stories. Now it's time to enter your own—not in theory, but in presence. Start small. Notice the room before you change it. Notice your breath before you speak. Notice your tone before you defend.

I use words like *alignment*, *awareness*, *congruence*, and *freedom*.

Those aren't abstractions; they're coordinates. Together, they point to a single destination: the ability to move through life without being split in two. To act, feel, and lead from the same source.

That's the work that remains.

So, pause for a moment. Take one slow breath. Feel the distance between where you are and who you could become. It's the same space I've lived in, coached in, fought in, and prayed in. It's where growth begins. Performance is simply the output of presence. And when you stop performing for approval and start performing from alignment, everything changes. Your relationships shift. Your team steadies. The air in the room gets clearer. You become the signal instead of the noise.

The most successful high achievers don't spend their lives chasing greatness. They embody it—quietly, daily—in the way they move, breathe, speak, recover, and begin again. So, ask yourself, where are you now, and what breakthrough would bring you closer to who you're capable of being? You don't need permission. You don't need another plan or another app. You don't need more motivation or a stronger why. You simply need awareness to see things as they are, followed by the courage to act on what it shows you. The rest will follow.

That's the Pressure Code—your personal Performance OS.

Now install it, live it, and return to your sweet spot. Not the one you chase when things are perfect but the one that sits just beneath the noise, waiting for you to quiet down long enough to feel it. You'll know it when you're there. It's that moment between inhale and exhale, when time slows, and the world stops demanding your attention. It's the space where effort and ease meet. You've been there before. It's the same pulse that shows up in a match, a conversation, a meeting, a walk in the dark when you stop trying to fix things and finally start listening again.

That's your reset point. The place where performance is the echo of alignment. Where everything you've built, every tool and principle, stops being theory and becomes muscle memory. It's the transition from thinking about the work to living it.

Living in coherence is always about truth. The truth of how your system wants to move when you stop forcing it. The truth that the pressure isn't ever going away—it just stops owning you. The truth that freedom is real and waiting to be earned, right here, in this breath, in this body, in this moment.

If you're stuck, you can always find that rhythm again. Not through striving, but through return. The real mark of mastery isn't how far you've gone, but how quickly you can come back when you drift. That's the takeaway I want you to remember: What separates the ones who burn out from the ones who keep building and succeeding is the ability to return to center, reset the system, and begin again.

That's what makes a champion and the promise of your potential fully realized.

That's your upgraded Performance OS, your code under pressure, your fuel for the spiral upward.

So, breathe.

Steady yourself.

And remember, in every aspect of the performance you seek, you already know the way forward.

Appendices—
The Performance OS Field Notes

What follows are the principles, practices, and reflections that run within your Pressure Code. They are a collection of tools that I've created for you to use when you feel off rhythm, when the system's lagging, or when you just want to fine-tune how you show up. Each section stands on its own: a quick recalibration you can run anytime the noise gets louder than the signal. Run them when you start to lag and revisit them after big wins or losses, or anytime you feel out of rhythm.

Use appendix I when you want tools for immediate traction.

Use appendix II when you want to dig deeper into the system's logic and principles.

Use appendix III when you need notes on perspective, or a reminder that even the people who teach this still practice it every day.

Together, they form a full loop: tools that reset the system, principles that explain it, and notes that humanize it.

Appendix I—The Tools

Performance OS Practices and Field Tests

Use the tools that follow when the day starts to spin, when the air in the room feels heavy, or when your own signal starts to fade. Some are highly specialized, and others are more general and overlapping. The point is, pick the tool that best helps you in the moment you need it.

WHAT YOU'LL FIND HERE

- The Fighter to Warrior Audit: Audit the gap between who shows up under pressure and who you want to be.
- The Daily Energy Ledger: Reveal where your energy actually goes, not where you think it should.
- Breathwork and Physiology Drills: The fastest way to change your emotional state is to change your physiology.
- The Weekly Energy Audit: Energy doesn't disappear; it just moves. This audit keeps you honest about where it's going and whether it's worth the cost.

- The Seven-Day Energy Stack: A weekly plan for combining breath, movement, and recovery practices.
- The Breath Reset: How to use breath to bring your body and focus back into sync.
- The Energy Audit: A simple way to spot where your energy is leaking and how to seal the holes.
- The Movement Reset: You can't think your way out of tension. You have to move through it.
- The Recovery Loop: Build recovery into the rhythm of your day.
- The Readiness Ritual: One minute of posture, breath, and focus.
- The SAVAGE Protocol: Something to hold on to when everything else is shaking.
- The Coherence Drill: When you're coherent, everything you are—breath, movement, intent—is pointed in the same direction.
- The Environmental Reset: How to read a room, recalibrate its tone, and bring yourself into alignment with it.

For additional tools, scan the QR code below (www.thepressurecode.com/start):

THE FIGHTER TO WARRIOR AUDIT

You can't change what you can't see.

This audit helps you identify which operating system runs when pressure is real—when stakes are high, time is short, and your margin for error disappears.

This is not a personality test.

It's a state audit.

Run it quarterly—or anytime you notice yourself slipping into urgency, reactivity, or grind mode.

HOW TO ANSWER

Answer each statement based on how you show up under pressure—not on your best days.

Think about:

- High-stakes meetings
- Conflict
- Fatigue
- Visibility
- When outcomes matter and recovery is limited

Use the scale below:

1 = Almost never under pressure
2 = Rarely
3 = Sometimes
4 = Often
5 = This is my default response when stressed

Answer quickly. Don't overthink it.

SECTION 1—FIGHTER ACTIVATION INDEX

How much threat, urgency, and control drive you under pressure.

Rate each statement 1–5:

1 = Never   2 = Rarely   3 = Sometimes   4 = Often   5 = Always

STATEMENT	SCORE (1-5)
I push through exhaustion even when my body is clearly depleted.	
I feel restless or irritated when progress slows or control slips.	
I rely on urgency, adrenaline, or pressure to stay focused.	
I react quickly before fully processing what's happening.	
I stay on guard because letting up feels risky.	
I take challenges or resistance personally.	
I struggle to downshift once I'm activated.	

Fighter Total: ____/ 35

SECTION 2—WARRIOR REGULATION INDEX

How well you regulate energy, emotions, and response under pressure.

Rate each statement 1–5:

1 = Never 2 = Rarely 3 = Sometimes 4 = Often 5 = Always

STATEMENT	SCORE (1-5)
I prepare for pressure instead of hoping I'll rise to it.	
I can shift gears—from calm to intensity and back—without losing control.	
I manage my energy deliberately, not just my output.	
I see adversity as training, not punishment.	
I stay grounded and respectful when things go sideways.	
I focus on rhythm and consistency, not just big wins.	
I know which principles I will not compromise—even under stress.	

Warrior Total: ____/ 35

INTERPRET YOUR RESULTS

Step 1: Identify your dominant mode. Compare your two totals:

- If your **Warrior score is higher**, you are **Warrior-dominant.**
- If your **Fighter score is higher**, you are **Fighter-dominant.**

Step 2: Calculate the difference. Subtract the smaller total from the larger one.

Difference Score = Higher total – Lower total
(This number will always be positive.)

Your result is determined by:

1. **Which mode is dominant.**
2. How large the gap is between them.

IF YOU ARE WARRIOR-DOMINANT

Difference of 0–4 → Mixed Code
You have access to Warrior skills, but under fatigue or surprise, Fighter habits still hijack control. Regulation is present—but inconsistent.

Difference of 5–14 → Warrior Emerging
You pause before reacting. Regulation is improving. Fighter energy still shows up under sustained stress, but it no longer runs the system.

Difference of 15+ → Warrior
Preparation, principle, and rhythm are your default. Pressure

sharpens you instead of destabilizing you. Fighter energy is available—but governed.

IF YOU ARE FIGHTER-DOMINANT

Difference of 0–4 → Mixed Code
You shift between awareness and reactivity. Sometimes you regulate well—sometimes urgency takes over. Consistency is the opportunity.

Difference of 5–14 → Fighter Dominant
High output, low recovery. You rely on intensity more than regulation. Sustainable in the short term—but costly over time.

Difference of 15+ → Stuck in Survival Mode
Threat and control drive behavior. Reactivity is the default. Regulation is largely unavailable when pressure hits.

REFLECTION PROMPTS

Take 10 minutes to answer the following prompts. Write fast, and don't edit as you go.

- Where in my life am I still fighting when preparation would serve me better?
- Which people, environments, or situations activate my Fighter most quickly?
- What signals does my body give me when I'm slipping into fight mode?
- What single daily action would strengthen my Warrior regulation?
- Who in my life already carries strong Warrior energy—and what do they do differently?

THE WARRIOR'S CODE—QUICK REFERENCE

PRINCIPLE	IN MODERN LIFE
Presence	Show up fully where your feet are.
Loyalty	Protect trust before chasing outcomes.
Discipline	Do what the moment demands, not what emotion wants.
Awareness (*zanshin*)	Stay alert before, during, and after the action.
Adaptability (*mushin*)	Let go of your attachment to results—stay fluid.
Courage	Face what you fear most with calm.
Stillness	Recovery is rhythm; that's where insight lives.

CLOSING NOTE

You can't control the fight, but you can control the code you're running when it begins.

- Fighters react to survive.
- Warriors prepare to serve.

Both a fighter and a warrior live inside you—but only one will help you build a system that lasts. Keep auditing the gap between who shows up under pressure and who you want to be.

THE DAILY ENERGY LEDGER

You likely know how to track time. But do you know how to track energy?

The daily energy ledger shows where your energy actually goes, not where you think it should. Use this tool to discover what you build, what you burn, and what you lose through leaks you never notice.

Why a ledger? When you treat energy like currency, every action, conversation, or environment becomes a deposit or a withdrawal. The goal isn't balance for balance's sake; it's awareness. Once you see the patterns, you have the information you need to intentionally choose (or reject) them.

CATEGORY	WHAT TO NOTE	EXAMPLE
Build (Deposits)	Moments, habits, or environments that restore or sharpen focus.	Early workout Quiet drive Clean workspace Time with family
Protect (Guard)	Boundaries that keep key energy sources from being drained.	Sleep window Recovery block Post-meeting decompression
Spend (Investments)	Where you'll direct focused energy today.	Key project High-stakes meeting Training session
Leak (Drains)	Small, repeated losses you tend to ignore.	Scattered multitasking Background noise Unfinished conversations
Balance (Reflection)	What built you? What drained you? What surprised you?	

At night, review the ledger. No judgment—just observation. Write or record what built you, what drained you, and what patterns you noticed. Do it for a week, and trends will start to show you which environments feed you, which people tax you, and how small adjustments have the power to compound results.

BREATHWORK AND PHYSIOLOGY DRILLS

ENERGY AND EMOTIONS IN MOTION

Breath is the body's reset button. When it gets shallow, speed takes over. When it steadies, awareness returns. The fastest way to change your emotional state is to change your physiology. You don't need a meditation cushion or a quiet room. You just need awareness and a few patterns that train your body to switch gears on command.

1. BREATHING FOR CONTROL

When you're amped, anxious, or overstimulated, you need down-regulation:

- Sit or stand tall.
- Roll your shoulders back.
- Inhale through the nose for four seconds, hold for two, and then exhale through the mouth for six.

If that feels forced, shorten it, but keep the exhale longer than the inhale. The longer release signals safety to the body.

Run this for two minutes before a meeting, a match, or before you sleep. It lowers cortisol and brings your system back into rhythm faster than any mantra. You'll know it's working when your jaw loosens, your hearing sharpens, and your pulse drops a beat.

COACHING NOTE

If anxiety spikes and you need to calm the system quickly, use what researchers call a psychological sigh. Take a deep breath in, pause briefly, then take a second short inhale to fill the lungs the rest of the way. After that, exhale slowly with a sigh.

Research from Stanford has shown this pattern can reduce stress and anxiety faster than longer exhales alone.[14] I use this when someone is overamped, anxious, or carrying too much noise into a moment. Twenty to thirty seconds is usually enough to feel the shift.

2. BREATHING FOR DRIVE

Before high-intensity effort, the goal isn't calm—it's coherence. When you need focus and activation, use up-regulation:

- Inhale strongly through the nose for two seconds, and exhale sharply through the mouth for another two seconds.
- Repeat that step 20 times.
- Take one long inhale, hold for 10 seconds, and exhale slowly.

This breathing exercise primes the system without tipping it into chaos. Use it before stepping into the arena, walking on stage, or taking the first serve.

3. SHIFTING STATES ON COMMAND

It's easy to toggle between getting overamped and staying underfired. Instead, learn to move between states deliberately.

- Start by identifying where you are: jittery or sluggish.
- If you're jittery, down-regulate with the 4-2-6 pattern.
    - Inhale through your nose for four seconds.
    - Hold for two seconds.
    - Exhale through your mouth for six seconds. The longer exhale triggers the parasympathetic response—the body's brake pedal—lowering your heart rate and calming excess adrenaline.
- If you're sluggish, up-regulate with the 2-2 pattern.
    - Inhale for two seconds, and exhale for two seconds to up-regulate. This increases alertness and oxygen flow, nudging the system back into readiness.
- Run each for 60 seconds and notice the shift in clarity. That's your Performance OS syncing in real time.

4. WEEKLY PROGRESSION

Here's a breakdown of what this would look like in a week.

- Days 1–2: Run down-regulation before sleep.
- Days 3–4: Use up-regulation before workouts or presentations.
- Day 5: Alternate patterns for contrast.
- Day 6: Run both exercises as the bookends of your day.
- Day 7: Skip the structure—just breathe and notice.

You're training your nervous system the same way you'd train any muscle: through reps, rest, and repetition.

COACHING NOTE

Every inhale activates the system. Every exhale regulates it. You can't think your way into balance; you have to breathe yourself there. Link this with your daily energy ledger. Run a quick entry before and after these drills and see how your energy scores shift. Over time, you'll stop needing the data—this level of awareness will become instinct.

THE WEEKLY ENERGY AUDIT

RHYTHM AND REFINEMENT

Most people drift without realizing it. The body starts compensating, the mind gets noisy, and by Friday, they're running on fumes. This audit is how you step back, see the patterns, and course-correct before burnout does it for you.

The daily energy ledger shows you where your power goes in a single day, but the weekly energy audit can show you how well you're managing it over time.

Think of this as a recovery ritual disguised as a review. You're not judging the week—you're studying it. Awareness always comes before adjustment.

STEP 1: CHOOSE THE WINDOW

Pick a 30-day block. Four weeks is long enough to see trends, but short enough to stay honest.

Every Sunday during that 30-day block, or whatever day you reset, take 10 quiet minutes to look at the week you just lived. Keep your daily energy ledgers close; they're the data underneath the reflection.

STEP 2: READ THE WEEK

Look for the rhythm, not the math.

- Which days felt lighter? Which dragged?
- Did energy drop with poor sleep, tough travel, toxic meetings, skipped recovery?
- Write down one line per day—a headline only you would understand:
    - Monday: solid flow after workout.
    - Wednesday: short fuse, no margin.
    - Friday: flat by noon.

Remember: You're tracing patterns more than collecting details.

STEP 3: MAP THE 3Es

Now, check your energy, emotions, and environment—the Performance OS's three layers.

- Score each E from 1 to 5 for the week.
- Write a short note under the lowest one. That's your system leak.

ELEMENT	SCORE (1-5)	QUICK NOTE
Energy		
Emotions		
Environment		

You'll start to see which layer keeps breaking the rhythm. Some people always burn out in energy; others collapse in emotions when their environment turns chaotic.

STEP 4: NAME THE LEAK

Don't rush to fix everything.

- Pick the single leak costing you the most. Maybe it's late-night screen time, overcommitting, skipping meals, or saying yes when you're empty.
- Write one sentence that defines it. That's your next week's mission.

STEP 5: APPLY THE UPGRADE

Choose one practical correction and run it for seven days. Small equals sustainable. For example, you could:

- Move your workout earlier in the day.
- Block out time for a 15-minute decompression walk.
- Clean your workspace every night.

Whatever you choose, track how it changes your 3E scores at the week's end. Remember, each micro-upgrade compounds.

STEP 6: RECALIBRATE

At the end of the 30-day cycle, read your notes out loud. You'll hear the shift before you see it. Your energy feels steadier. Your recovery comes faster. Your mood resets quicker. That's what rhythm sounds like.

If you're leading a team, do this together. Have each person share one energy win and one leak they're working on, helping to hold each other accountable. That conversation alone will change the culture.

COACHING NOTE

As we know from physics, energy doesn't disappear; it just shifts. This audit keeps you honest about where it's going and whether it's worth the cost. Treat it like a standing meeting with yourself. One that protects the only asset every performer shares: the power to stay steady when it matters most.

SEVEN-DAY ENERGY STACK

Energy isn't built in a single workout. It's trained, layer by layer, just like any other system. The body learns rhythm the same way it learns skill—through repetition, recovery, and awareness.

This seven-day stack is a calibration plan. It's not a challenge or a detox; it's a week of tuning the three main circuits of the Performance OS—breath, movement, and recovery—until they start talking to each other. By the end of the week, you'll start to feel the charge come back—steady, clean, usable.

DAY 1—BASELINE

Start simple.

- Morning: Take 10 nasal breaths—four-second inhale, eight-second exhale.
- Evening: Take a 20-minute walk without your phone. Notice your posture and breath. Let the day fall away.

This is your baseline. No judgment, just noticing how your system feels when you're not forcing anything.

DAY 2—CO_2 TOLERANCE

This trains you to stay calm under discomfort.

- Drill: Exhale fully. Hold the exhale until the urge to breathe rises, then recover slowly. Do this for three rounds.
- Integration: Practice the holds while walking at an easy pace.

This teaches your body what stress really feels like—and how to stay relaxed inside it.

DAY 3—RECOVERY RESET

Pressure without recovery is corrosion.

- Practice: Complete two short reset loops—roll, breathe, set, aim—before lunch, then two more in the afternoon.
- Evening: Turn the lights down an hour earlier. No screens.

You're teaching your system that rest is part of work, not the absence of it.

DAY 4—MOVEMENT INTEGRATION

Energy moves through the body, not around it.

- Morning: Get in 15 minutes of easy motion. This can be through a walk, stretch, or bodyweight flow.

- Throughout the day: Every 90 minutes, complete two minutes of movement to change state.

Each reset reminds the nervous system it has options besides "on" and "off."

DAY 5—FOCUS EXPANSION

Awareness isn't focus—it's control of focus.

- Drill: Box breathing—four breaths in, hold for four counts, breathe out for four, hold for four again (four equal sides, which is why it's called a box)—for five minutes.
- Practice: During one task, watch your four dials: arousal, attention, focus, and intensity. Adjust one of them using the framework outlined in chapter 4.

This builds the muscle of selective awareness, teaching you to choose what deserves your full power.

DAY 6—EXTENDED HOLD

Endurance is quiet control.

- Drill: After a full exhale, hold while walking 10 steps. Repeat three to five times.
- Evening: Write down three leaks you protected against this week.

This is how you train integrity—keeping energy where it belongs.

DAY 7—AUDIT AND ALIGN

The final day is reflection, not rest.

- Audit: Review your deposits, leaks, and spends. Where did rhythm hold? Where did it break?
- Ritual: 20-minute descent practice—close open loops, plan tomorrow's first move, turn the lights down.

By the end of those seven days, you'll have more than a stack—you'll have a rhythm you can repeat. The body now knows what alignment feels like. Keep running this loop until the pattern becomes reflex: Breathe, move, recover, repeat.

THE BREATH RESET

When I first started working with athletes, I thought breathwork was about oxygen. Now I know it's actually about awareness. The breath is the body's report card—it tells you what the nervous system already knows, but the ego refuses to admit.

A boxer before a title fight once asked me, "What should I focus on in the first round?"

I said, "Your breath. If you can feel it, you're still in control."

He nodded as if he understood. He didn't. No one really does until the moment hits. Pressure compresses everything: vision, hearing, judgment. The body starts to sprint while the mind tries to think. That's the split that breaks people. Breath is what stitches it back together.

HOW THE RESET WORKS

There's no trademarked routine here—just rhythm. The key is to restore rhythm before you restore logic.

1. Start by noticing the breath you're already taking. Don't fix it yet. Just listen. Is it high in the chest? Fast? Tight? That's the nervous system talking.
2. Then anchor it. Place a hand over the diaphragm—right below the ribs—and breathe so that your hand rises before your chest does.
3. Breathe in for four counts. Breathe out for six. Nothing fancy. The longer exhale lowers the arousal level. You're telling the body, *We're safe enough to focus again.*
4. Once you can control one breath, control three.
5. Then five.
6. After that, awareness returns.

BEFORE THE MATCH OR MEETING

Every environment has its own energy signature—stadiums, boardrooms, even the living room before a hard conversation. The trick isn't to fight that energy; it's to sync your system before you enter it.

Here are the instructions I give to my players and executives before they walk into high-stakes moments:

1. Release two deep exhales. Empty the lungs to clear static.
2. Take three steady breaths in through the nose and out through the mouth. Make them slow and intentional.
3. Take one short power inhale through the nose and one sharp exhale through the mouth. That's how you switch to calm and ready.

The whole sequence takes less than a minute, but I've seen it change the outcome of entire matches, board presentations, and family dinners.

WHY IT WORKS

Most people think regulation is mental. It's not. It's mechanical.

The vagus nerve runs through the diaphragm; when the diaphragm moves, the nervous system listens. Breath tells the body to downshift, which tells the brain it can stop scanning for threats.

That's why recovery doesn't start when the game ends; it starts with the first controlled exhale under pressure. The masters I've coached—athletes, soldiers, CEOs—don't have more discipline; they have faster recovery. They close the gap between stress and regulation until it's invisible. That's what the breath reset does. It shrinks that gap.

THE FIELD TEST

Try this tomorrow morning. Before checking your phone, sit on the edge of your bed. Place one hand on your chest and the other on your stomach.

- Complete three rounds of breathing in for four seconds and out for six.
- Then ask yourself one question: *What's the signal I want to send today?*

Your breath will tell you if you're aligned. If you're rushing or holding, the system already knows you're off. If it's smooth, even for a few seconds, that's coherence and control.

THE ENERGY AUDIT

When people burn out, they always think it's about time.

It's not.

It's about energy—how they spend it, how they lose it, and whether the environment they're in ever gives any back. I started noticing this years ago when I was coaching players on tour. Two athletes could train for the same number of hours, eat the same food, even travel the same schedule, but one would stay steady while the other would unravel. The difference wasn't work ethic; it was leakage. One knew how to hold energy, the other didn't.

Energy leaks are quiet. They hide in habits that feel productive: endless planning, background worry, unfinished conversations you keep replaying. You don't feel the cost until your focus goes thin and you start resenting the things you used to love.

MAPPING THE FLOW

Before you can manage energy, you have to see it. That's what the audit is for. You don't need a spreadsheet, just awareness.

1. For one week, carry a small notebook or open a note on your phone.
2. After every major block of your day—a meeting, a workout, a call—name the event and write one line: Did that give me energy or take it?
3. Don't judge the answer. Just collect it.

Patterns will show up fast. You'll see which people steady you and which leave you buzzing or drained. You'll see which kinds of work fill you up and which strip you down. Remember, awareness applies pressure. The moment you start seeing, your system starts to recalibrate.

THE INVISIBLE DRAINS

Most leaks aren't dramatic. They're friction—small misalignments that multiply.

For one client, it was the five minutes before every Zoom call when he'd check emails and doomscroll news headlines. It spiked his nervous system, and he'd enter meetings already reactive. For another, it was skipping his post-training cool-down to answer messages. The body never learned to close the stress loop, so recovery never started.

These sound minor, but they're not. Energy is cumulative. Every unclosed loop adds load to the system until you're carrying more tension than your awareness can track.

RECLAIMING THE CHARGE

Once you can see the leaks, you can start sealing them. Here's how.

- Single-focus moments: Give one thing your full attention until it's done. The nervous system loves completion.
- Micro-resets: Every two hours, do one minute of slow breathing or walking. That single minute prevents fatigue from compounding.
- Boundary rituals: Turn travel time, commutes, or short walks into transition points. Exhale the last role before you enter the next.

The point isn't discipline for its own sake. It's rhythm. Energy doesn't need constant management; it needs predictable release and recovery.

THE THREE R'S OF ALIGNMENT

When I teach this in workshops, I simplify it into a loop: recognize, regulate, rebuild.

- Recognize the leak—notice the moment your body tightens or your tone sharpens.
- Regulate—one slow breath, one deliberate pause.
- Rebuild—move, stretch, hydrate, reset posture to reconnect with purpose.

Most people try to skip rebuilding. They add supplements, vacations, another hack. None of it works if you haven't recognized or regulated first. Awareness before action—that's the operating system.

THE FIELD TEST

Tomorrow, run a quiet experiment. At the end of your day, create two columns:

- What fueled me?
- What drained me?

Answer both questions honestly. Then, circle one fuel and one drain you can act on tomorrow.

You don't have to fix everything; you just have to shift the ratio of things that fuel you and things that drain you. If you do that for a week, the pattern becomes clear. Alignment isn't a state you chase; it's a balance you maintain.

THE MOVEMENT RESET

When I was younger, I thought rest meant stopping. Now I know the body never stops—it just changes states. Movement isn't exercise; it's information. It tells you where tension lives and what your system is trying to protect.

I started realizing this when I watched players after a loss. They'd pace, stretch, bounce, or drop their head into their hands. Each pattern was the body trying to process what the mind couldn't. The athletes who recovered fastest weren't the ones who analyzed—they were the ones who moved with awareness.

Your body remembers everything your mind tries to skip over. When you change your physical pattern, you change the story your nervous system is telling. That's the movement reset.

WHY IT MATTERS

Stillness has its place, but under pressure it can turn into stagnation. If breath resets awareness, movement resets emotion. It gives the body permission to release charge, reorient, and start again.

Elite performers live in their heads until they can't feel the signal anymore. They train thought and execution, forgetting that the body is the first part of the system to go offline. When you move with intention—walk, hinge, rotate, breathe—you resync the physical and mental OS.

You can't think your way out of tension. You have to move through it.

HOW THE RESET WORKS

Use this anytime you feel the signal drop—after long focus, after conflict, or when fatigue turns to frustration. It only takes three minutes:

1. Stand and ground: Feet flat, knees soft, weight even. Feel the floor under you. One full breath in through the nose, long exhale through the mouth.
2. Hinge: Fold forward at the hips, letting your arms hang. Release the neck. Three slow breaths here. Let gravity stretch the backline.
3. Rotate: Slowly roll up. Sweep your arms side to side, turning from the torso; eyes following your hands. Keep the movement easy.
4. Reach and breathe: Inhale as you lift your arms overhead; exhale as you lower them. Feel the ribs expand.
5. Recenter: Come back to stillness. Keep your eyes level and release one long exhale.

Three minutes for a full reboot. You've just closed an emotional loop your body was carrying for hours.

FIELD APPLICATION

Before a meeting, between sets, after an argument, movement is the nervous system's language for expressing *We're okay again*. When you teach the body to find flow again, the mind follows. Your awareness widens. Your emotions stabilize. Effort starts to feel clean.

THE FIELD TEST

Next time you feel yourself tightening—hands clenching, shoulders rising, jaw locking—pause and run the movement reset. Don't call it a stretch; call it a systems check. If your body loosens, your focus returns, and your breath deepens, you've just witnessed coherence in motion. That's the point.

THE RECOVERY LOOP

Early in my career, I treated recovery like a reward—something you earned after pushing hard enough. That was a mistake. Recovery isn't what you do after the work. It's what keeps the work sustainable.

The best performers I've ever coached don't just train better—they recover more quickly. They don't wait for burnout to force them to stop. They build recovery into the rhythm of their day, so the system never collapses under the load. The recovery loop helps you do just that. It's a way to finish strong and stay steady.

WHY IT MATTERS

Most people confuse recovery with rest. They collapse at the end of the day and call it recovery. Rest is passive. Recovery is active; it's awareness in motion. You can't separate performance from recovery. They're part of the same loop—one expands capacity, the other restores it. When the loop breaks, the system starts leaking. Reaction times slow, emotional bandwidth shrinks, and mistakes multiply. Rebuilding the loop means learning to downshift on command, not when exhaustion forces it.

The loop is simple: Roll, breathe, set, aim.

ROLL

Let go of the task in front of you. Physically release it:

- Open your hands.
- Roll your shoulders back and down.
- Open your chest.
- Breathe out through your mouth like you're clearing smoke.

BREATHE

Take two slow inhales through the nose and one long exhale through the mouth. Feel your nervous system slide down a gear.

SET

Reset your posture. Realign your stance. Check in: *Is your attention where you need it next?*

AIM

Before moving forward, set one small target. Not ten. One. That single point of focus keeps your mind anchored when energy is low.

This whole sequence takes less than a minute. You can run it between calls, after workouts, or when you catch yourself grinding without presence.

THE FIELD TEST

Run the recovery loop twice in the morning and twice in the afternoon. Notice what happens when you close the gap between effort and recovery.

If your focus sharpens and your body stops fighting itself, the loop is working. That's coherence.

THE READINESS RITUAL

Motivation is emotional. Readiness is structural. Most people wait to feel ready before they move. Elite performers move first and let readiness catch up. They don't rely on adrenaline or hype. They build a system that cues them into focus, whether they're ready or not.

That's what the readiness ritual does. It's a simple framework to prepare the body, clear the mind, and steady your emotions before you step into a high-pressure situation.

WHY IT MATTERS

Motivation burns fast. It's built on emotion, and emotion changes by the hour. Readiness runs deeper. It's built on rhythm.

When your system knows what readiness feels like, you can summon it on demand. That's what separates professionals from amateurs—consistency of state. If recovery keeps you from breaking down, readiness keeps you from freezing up.

The ritual has three checkpoints: ready body, clear mind, steady emotions.

1. READY BODY

Start by aligning your posture and breath:

- Stand tall with soft knees and a level chin.
- Inhale for four counts; exhale for six.
- Feel your feet under you.

Readiness starts from the ground up—if your body's anchored, the rest will follow.

2. CLEAR MIND

Once the body is ready, you need to clear your mental clutter. Ask yourself: *What actually matters in the next 10 minutes?* Not the outcome. Not the noise. Just the next action that moves you forward.

Focus shrinks anxiety. When your mind has a single target, pressure has nowhere to live.

3. STEADY EMOTIONS

The final cue is emotional tone.

- Check your internal volume. Too high, you'll force it. Too low, you'll drift.
- Adjust with breath. Release long exhales for calm. Take quick breaths for activation.

This is emotional regulation in real time. You're not trying to control how you feel; you're tuning it to match what's required.

THE FIELD TEST

Tomorrow morning, before you check your phone or open your laptop, stand still and run through the three checkpoints: ready body, clear mind, steady emotions.

See how that changes the first 10 minutes of your day.

Then try it again before your next high-stakes moment—a meeting, a call, a workout. When readiness becomes your default state, motivation becomes optional. You don't wait to feel right, you just act. And that's how the system stays ready—no matter what it walks into.

THE SAVAGE PROTOCOL

Pressure doesn't care how prepared you are. It will always find the crack in your system. The question isn't whether you'll feel it—it's what you do next.

The SAVAGE Protocol was born out of those moments when everything starts to spin: a match point, a boardroom question you didn't see coming, a family crisis you can't walk away from. It's a step-by-step reset for when the body locks up and the mind goes blank.

The acronym isn't bravado. It's a reminder: See. Assess. Validate. Adjust. Ground. Execute.

WHY IT MATTERS

Under pressure, your awareness collapses. Your vision narrows, your breath shortens, and your instinct turns reactive. The nervous system is built for survival, not precision. The SAVAGE Protocol widens that awareness again. It gives your system something to hold onto when everything else is shaking.

This is not a breathing drill. It's a command sequence—a way to bring order back to chaos in real time. You can run it in 15 seconds or three minutes. Use it any time pressure spikes and your system starts to fragment.

S—SEE

Step back; pause. Look at what's actually in front of you. Not the outcome, not the fear, not the future—just the one frame you're in.

A—ASSESS

Ask yourself: *What's real right now?* Strip away assumptions. Clarity starts when you stop fighting shadows.

V—VALIDATE

Name what you're feeling without judgment. Tension, frustration, panic—it's data, not weakness. Labeling emotions calms the nervous system by giving it language.

A—ADJUST

One slow breath. One posture change. One small correction in tone or timing. Micro-adjustments reassert control faster than massive overhauls.

G—GROUND

Feel your feet. Exhale through the mouth. Grounding signals to your body, *We're back.*

E—EXECUTE

Make the next clear move. Don't chase perfection; chase precision.

THE FIELD TEST

Next time your pulse spikes and you feel the static rise, run the letters in your head: See. Assess. Validate. Adjust. Ground. Execute.

Repeat these steps out loud under your breath if you have to. Slow down until you can feel each one land. You'll know it's working when your vision widens, your breath deepens, and time feels slower again. That's coherence returning—the system reestablishing order. The SAVAGE Protocol transforms pressure into presence.

THE COHERENCE DRILL

There's a moment in every performance—on the court, in the meeting, in life—where everything tightens. The breath shortens. The eyes dart. You lose the rhythm that was there a second ago. That's fragmentation. But coherence brings it back. Coherence means your body, emotions, and attention stop fighting each other and move in the same direction again.

WHY IT MATTERS

It's one thing to chase calm under pressure. Calm is nice, but it's not the goal. Calm can be passive. Coherence is active.

When you're coherent, every breath, movement, and intention is pointed in the same direction. You're fully engaged without being hijacked. You're present but not frozen. That's what elite performance feels like. Not relaxed—integrated.

HOW THE DRILL WORKS

This takes just five minutes. Do it before a big moment, or any time you feel yourself drifting.

1. Stand and breathe: Feet flat, knees soft, chin level. Inhale through the nose for four counts; exhale through the mouth for six. Feel the ground under you. That's your baseline.
2. Align the frame: Roll your shoulders back. The crown of your head should be rising as if from a string. Let your posture stack naturally—feet, hips, ribs, shoulders, head. Alignment starts physically before it ever becomes mental.
3. Set the gaze: Pick a fixed point in front of you. Let your eyes rest there. Don't stare. Notice how your breath and focus begin to synchronize.
4. Scan for tension: From your jaw to your toes, find one area of tightness. Exhale directly into it until it releases.
5. Sync the system:
    - Inhale: feel your energy rise.
    - Exhale: feel your system settle.
6. Repeat until your breath, posture, and awareness feel like one motion.

This is the physical experience of coherence—the system running cleanly, without internal resistance.

FIELD APPLICATION

You can use this anywhere: backstage, in the tunnel before a match, or alone in your car before a hard conversation. It takes less time than a text message. One of my clients, a CEO, runs this drill before every all-hands meeting.

He told me, "It's not about calming down anymore. It's about tuning in." When the body becomes the tuning fork, the room adjusts around it.

THE FIELD TEST

Tomorrow, set a timer for five minutes.

Stand still. Breathe. Align.

Notice when your thoughts and breath start to move at the same speed. That's your signal. When you reach coherence, you'll feel a quiet kind of power—not intensity, not excitement, just clarity.

THE ENVIRONMENTAL RESET

You can walk into a room and feel everything that's being said before a word is spoken. The posture, the tone, the silence between sounds—all of it tells you what's really happening. Most people sense it and move on. Performers read it and reset it.

Your environment is what you allow into where you are. Every space carries a charge. That charge either supports you or drains you. The environmental reset is about taking back authorship of that charge, whether it's physical, social, or emotional.

STEP ONE: READ THE ROOM

Before you try to control anything, just notice it. The first 30 seconds in any environment will give you more data than the next 30 minutes.

- What's the sound level?
- What's the pace?
- Who's driving the energy?
- Where's the tension hiding?

Don't fix it yet. Just map it. Awareness alone starts shifting the signal.

If the air feels heavy, it usually means people are guarding. If it feels chaotic, the group's missing focus. If it feels flat, someone's not being honest.

Those aren't problems you need to try to solve immediately. For now, they're just indicators.

STEP TWO: ADJUST YOUR OWN SIGNAL

Every environment has a dominant frequency. You can either join it or influence it. And influence always starts with coherence.

Check your own system before you try to change the room:

- Is your breathing steady?
- Is your posture open or defensive?
- Is your tone matching your intention?

The room takes its cue from you, not your words. Change your state, and the environment follows. Sometimes it means:

- Softening your tone when tension rises.
- Raising your energy when the space feels dead.
- Being silent until the noise runs out.

Awareness first, adjustment second.

STEP THREE: CALIBRATE THE SPACE

Once you're stable, make one small physical change that signals a reset:

- Open a curtain.
- Shift the seating pattern.
- Lower the music or turn it off.
- Stand instead of sit.
- Bring fresh air into the room.

These tiny environmental cues tell the nervous system that something has changed. The shift doesn't have to be dramatic; it just needs to be intentional.

STEP FOUR: PROTECT THE RESET

The environment will always drift back to entropy unless you protect the tone you've set.

In team spaces, that means reinforcing rhythm:

- consistent start times
- shared rituals
- common breathing before action

In personal spaces, it means building micro-moments of order:

- a clear desk before bed
- sunlight in the morning
- a few deep breaths before opening your phone

Those are control points. They keep the operating system stable under load.

THE FIELD TEST

Tomorrow, walk into every room like a reader. Before you speak, take one slow breath and scan: What's the signal here, and what's mine?

Then, make one small change—a gesture, a tone, a question, a light. Watch what happens. By the end of the day, you'll see that leadership has less to do with authority and more to do with atmosphere.

You don't always get to choose the room you walk into, but you can always choose the energy you bring with you. And if you do that consistently, the room eventually starts choosing you.

Appendix II—The Principles Behind the Practice

Deeper Reflections on the 3Es

The Performance OS isn't a magic fix-all solution. It's physics, chemistry, and awareness operating in sync. It's only when you start seeing the patterns under the practice that you can start mastering systems. Each essay in this section opens a window to one of the three Es—energy, emotions, environment—shedding light on how they merge into coherence through lived experience.

WHAT YOU'LL FIND HERE

- The Science of Scent: How emotions move chemically through space and why the air in a room can change performance before a word is spoken.
- Through Loyalty: The chemistry of trust, and how loyalty stabilizes energy, anchors teams, and builds freedom through reliability.
- Culture by Design: How environments grow up and become culture.

- The Leadership Environment Map: How your state becomes the system.
- The Performance Ecosystem: How energy, emotions, and environment work as one system.
- The Silent Spread: How emotions transfer through breathing, posture, and presence before words are spoken.
- Leaking Versus Charging: Why you're tired before you should be, and what's draining you without your permission.
- You Don't Just Live in Environments, They Live in You: How physical, social, and psychological spaces shape your state before you act.
- Why Certain Rooms Make You Small (and How to Reclaim Them): Environmental intimidation, emotional memory, and the warrior approach to space ownership.

Together, they explain why awareness alone isn't enough. You need structure, chemistry, and rhythm to make lasting changes to your life.

THE SCIENCE OF SCENT

ENVIRONMENT AS CHEMISTRY

You can feel a room before you can describe it. Walk into a locker room, a meeting, or a home after an argument, and the air has weight. Nobody has to speak to communicate it. Your breath catches in your chest. The rhythm has changed.

Emotion travels faster than thought. It rides on molecules. When someone walks into a room, angry or calm, your nervous system reacts to the scent before your mind understands. The limbic system—the part of the brain tied to emotion and memory—sits one step from the nose. You smell how someone feels before you can name what you feel.

In performance, that signal matters. If the air carries anxiety, bodies tighten before anyone notices. A team starts mirroring the same chemical field. They breathe stress and call it focus.

When I coach, I pay attention to the air first. Is it thick or light? Sharp or steady? Does it smell like effort or tension? Before anyone touches a racket or a weight, I tell the room to exhale. Sometimes that means opening a window. Sometimes that means 10 slow breaths together. Change the air, and you change what the body believes.

Recovery spaces do the same thing. Scent sets the nervous system's tempo. It can steady awareness or scatter it. One calm breath can shift the whole room. The body keeps signaling; the group keeps responding. When one person settles, everyone breathes a little deeper.

Performance is closely tied to your atmosphere, but you can't control every single molecule. Instead, just try to *notice* them. The moment the air shifts, ask what you're bringing into it. Because the room always knows before you do.

THROUGH LOYALTY

ENERGY AS TRUST

My old sensei used to say, "Through loyalty, you gain trust. With trust comes freedom. To maintain that freedom, remain loyal."

I heard those words long before I ever coached anyone, but they've become integral to my coaching practice. Back then, it sounded like a model of discipline, but years later, I understood that it was chemistry.

Loyalty is more than a feeling; it's an energy current between people. When someone knows you'll show up the same way every time—steady, calm, honest—their system relaxes. Energy stops leaking. That's what trust feels like at the cellular level: predictability in motion.

The week before Wimbledon, Aryna suffered a weird injury. Her shoulder was done . . . no overhead and nobody could tell us how or why. We went to Wimbledon to see what we could do. Could she play? Should she play? Were we pulling out? She was the favorite to win, and everything was going well. Sitting in the doctor's office, I told her she *must* pull out. She started to get upset, but I stopped her and said, "You don't have to believe me. I'm asking you to trust me."

Belief comes later, after the proof—trust is what bridges the unknown. It's the signal that says, "You can stay present here."

On every team, trust works like breath. When it's shallow, tension builds. When it's steady, rhythm returns. People will move as one when their energy fields sync up. You can't fake that alignment; you earn it through reliability. Loyalty is the stabilizer, keeping energy anchored so creativity and freedom can exist without chaos.

That's why loyalty isn't blind obedience. It means holding form when the environment shakes, showing up the same when things get hard, and giving others space to breathe because they know you're stable.

Freedom doesn't come from control. It comes from a trust strong enough to let go.

CULTURE BY DESIGN

DESIGN OR DRIFT

It still surprises me how quickly you can read a culture by its air. You don't need a survey. You don't need a mission statement framed on the wall. Just stand there for 30 seconds and breathe. The air will tell you everything you need to know.

Some places hum with movement, people speaking in full sentences, and laughter in the corners. In other places, the air feels dense. You can feel it weighing on you the second you step into the room. You can sense fatigue, the kind that builds up when people care but no longer believe they can change anything.

Culture grows out of those invisible pressures. It's the environment, scaled. It's what happens when the habits, tone, and energy of a leader multiply across a hundred small interactions until they take on a life of their own. And culture won't wait for your permission. It starts forming the moment two people share the same space. Whether you mean to or not, you're always building toward something.

I used to think culture was personality—get the right mix of talent, values, and slogans and everything clicks. But personality without design drifts. It becomes reactive, bending to whatever force is loudest that week. The teams that sustain performance don't rely on charisma or luck; they engineer rhythm. They build rituals that carry meaning even when the leader isn't in the room.

That's why I tell leaders that if it's not in the calendar, it's not in the culture.

If trust matters, show me where it lives in your week.

If recovery matters, show me the boundary that protects it.

If reflection matters, show me the time and space where it's allowed to happen.

The calendar is a mirror. It reflects your real priorities, not the ones you print on slides. And it's the simplest diagnostic tool I know. Pull up any team's schedule, and you'll see what it worships. Meetings that never end? The culture worships control. Constant reschedules? The culture is overrun by chaos. Empty space for thinking? That's a team that values clarity over noise.

Culture is never neutral. It's always teaching something—patience or panic, trust or fear, speed or depth. You can tell what's being taught by what gets repeated, rewarded, or quietly tolerated. The repetition is the curriculum.

I've seen leaders try to fix culture by rewriting values. They roll out new language, host town halls, change the posters hanging in the training rooms. But culture is like the weather, and the first priority is changing the temperature inside when the temperature is rising outside. Shift how people feel when they walk in the door, what they expect from silence, and how they recover from failure. Once the air changes, the words start to mean something again.

Rebuilding culture always begins with a physical shift. In my work, this has been as small a change as rearranging where people sit, such as removing desks or physical barriers between departments, and scrapping meetings that have outlived their usefulness. The body feels a space before the mind explains it. Once the space breathes, behavior follows.

And yet, design isn't about control. It's about alignment. The best cultures run on shared rhythm. The leader sets the initial beat, but the team keeps time. Over the years, that rhythm becomes identity—the unspoken rules about how you treat people, how you handle conflict, what you chase, and what you refuse to trade away.

I've walked into companies where the air told me I was in the presence of something real. Not perfect, mind you, but real. You could feel care and clarity existing in the same room, which is rare. You could sense the loyalty that comes from people who've suffered together but never stopped showing up for each other. That kind of culture is earned, molecule by molecule, breath by breath.

So, when I talk about culture by design, I'm not talking about perfection. I'm talking about intention—about refusing to let the worst habits win by default. Culture doesn't need a hero; it needs a gardener. Someone patient enough to prune and stubborn enough to keep planting even when the season turns against them.

Which is why I say that culture is just environment over time, when design hardens into a pattern. You can let that process drift, or you can steer it. You can let the air go stale, or you can open a window. But one way or another, the air will teach. It always does.

THE LEADERSHIP ENVIRONMENT MAP

YOUR STATE BECOMES THE SYSTEM

Your nervous system teaches everyone else how to behave. Whatever state you're in—calm or scattered, grounded or reactive—becomes the baseline the team calibrates to. If you're clear, people borrow that clarity. If you're rushed, they speed up. If you're anxious, the entire room tightens its breath to match yours. The body is constantly broadcasting, and people are constantly listening.

I learned this lesson years ago, working with an athlete who could light up a training session just by walking in. She had presence—not because she was loud or charismatic, but because her internal system was clean. She carried order into every space she entered. You could see it in the way she tied her shoes, in the rhythm of her breath before a serve. When she was calm, the room followed her. When she wobbled, everything else did too. It's the same with leadership. Your body is the first system everyone else syncs to, whether you mean to lead with it or not.

That's what I mean when I say your state becomes the system. It's not metaphorical. The internal—your breath, tone, energy—sets the conditions for the external. The space you shape, the behaviors you model, and the culture that grows from both all trace back to the same signal—you. The best leaders understand this chain intuitively, even if they never name it. They can sense when the loop is clean and when it's not. They notice how the internal state flows outward into behavior, how behavior sets the atmosphere, and how atmosphere, over time, becomes culture.

But most drift without realizing it. They start grounded, centered, and clear on their purpose, but then the noise begins. The meetings stack, the decisions pile up, the pressure builds. Slowly, their nervous system slips from steady to strained. They start reacting instead of leading. And because the state is contagious, that strain becomes the new normal. Teams begin to mirror the same habits—shorter attention spans, shallow listening, rushed decisions. What used to feel fluid turns mechanical.

The good news is that drift is reversible. Sometimes it's one deep breath. Sometimes it's stepping outside for two minutes of quiet before walking into a high-stakes conversation. Whatever the method, the point is to reassert coherence before you infect the room with your chaos.

We talk about culture as if it's external, something you build outside yourself. But it's more accurate to think of it as an echo. What begins inside a leader reverberates through tone, behavior, and, eventually, policy. A leader's internal environment becomes the organization's external reality. That's why sustainable culture isn't about slogans or strategies; it's about regulated systems. When leaders lose touch with their own coherence, they unconsciously build structures that mirror that disarray.

THE PERFORMANCE ECOSYSTEM

THE LOOP

Performance isn't a set of separate levers. It's a living field—energy, emotions, and environment feeding one another in a constant loop. You can't isolate one without changing the others. The body knows this even when the mind doesn't. You've felt it. A single hard conversation drains your focus for hours, or a cluttered space turns a good morning sour before it begins. One variable shifts, and the entire system reacts.

Energy is the currency: what emotions spend and environments collect. Every day, you're making invisible transactions—what you give, what you absorb, and what you waste by resisting what's already true.

Emotions are the signal. They tell you how the system is reading the world.

The environment is the amplifier. It doesn't create who you are—it reveals and repeats it.

When the three align—energy clean, emotions steady, environment coherent—you can feel it. The real work of elite performance isn't to stay perfect; it's to recover fast. You don't prevent drift—you prepare for it. You build systems that find their way back to coherence faster every time they fall out of it.

The Pressure Code was built to restore that balance. It's not a productivity framework or a leadership formula—it's a language for coherence. It teaches you to see the feedback loop that's already running: Emotions shaping energy, energy shaping environment, environment shaping emotions. Round and round. When the loop's clean, performance feels like music. When it's noisy, it feels like static.

This is probably counterintuitive, but leadership is less about managing outcomes and more about tending ecosystems—listening to what each part needs to stay alive. Do that, and the outcomes naturally follow.

But it's not easy. You have to let the system breathe, trusting that if you keep energy clean, emotions honest, and environment intentional, the rest will take care of itself. It's a big ask, especially the way we train leaders today. But what I've learned in some of the most challenging performance environments in the world is that the system *will* learn—if you allow it.

THE SILENT SPREAD

WHAT YOU BROADCAST

You don't have to say a word for people to feel your emotional state. Pressure, anxiety, frustration, panic, calm, confidence, focus, fear, and certainty are contagious nervous system signals.

In high-performance environments—from locker rooms to boardrooms to corners during a fight—the emotional tone of just one individual can elevate or destabilize the entire group. This is why warriors control their emotional signals. They've learned that emotional states are not private—they radiate and affect those around them.

CHANNEL	HOW IT TRANSMITS	EXAMPLE
Breathing	Pace and depth impact others' breathing subconsciously.	One person panicking makes others speed up.
Posture	Slumped or tense posture signals defeat or fear.	Team sees shoulders collapse and morale drops.
Presence/ Facial Tone	Eye tension Jaw lock Gaze intensity	A calm gaze in chaos stabilizes others. Darting eyes create shared panic.

Emotions silently spread via three major channels. This is part of polyvagal co-regulation as human nervous systems constantly read each other's safety or threat signals without conscious intention. If you leak panic, others will feel it—even before you speak.

- In a crisis discussion, if you exhale sharply, flatten your head posture, and blink rapidly, others will unconsciously brace for danger.

- If you're leading a team and your voice carries a hidden tremor, tension spreads like static.
- In a match, when your shoulders rise and your breathing quickens, your opponent feels your instability—not because they notice, but because their nervous system feels it.

But the same is true for calm, focus, and composure.

- A leader who breathes low and slow creates psychological room for others to think clearly.
- A coach who maintains relaxed readiness under pressure gives the team permission to stay composed.
- A fighter who steps back with controlled breathing after being hit signals they're not shaken. The opponent feels that.

This is why warriors don't just control emotion—they transmit alignment.

WHY THIS MATTERS IN LEADERSHIP, COACHING, AND HIGH-STAKES TEAMS

PERFORMER TYPE	BEHAVIOR WHEN STRESSED	IMPACT ON TEAM
Fighter Mindset	Shows intensity, panic, or aggression	Creates a tension ripple
Warrior Mindset	Shows grounded, controlled threat-readiness	Creates a stability ripple

The warrior doesn't need everyone to be calm. They need to focus on themselves and ensure that they are unshakable enough to become the stable point around which others steady themselves. This doesn't mean suppressing emotion—it means signaling strength.

You don't have to hide fear—you have to lead the energy.

You don't have to be emotionless—you have to be intentionally readable.

You don't have to fake confidence—you have to transmit composure you've earned through self-control.

ELEMENT	WHAT CHANGES
Energy	You understand nervous systems sync, so control is multiplied.
Emotions	You no longer see it as personal—you see it as directional energy.
Environment	You can now shape the emotional climate instead of being shaped by it.
Warrior Identity	You step into the role of emotional stabilizer, not emotional reactor.

FIELD NOTE

There have been times when I'm coaching Aryna that she's walked onto the court in a way that the opponent could *feel* her presence, her calm force. That emotional signal was often the first win of the match.

CLOSING SHIFT

You are never just managing your emotions—you are broadcasting them. Warriors understand that emotional regulation is not just for survival but for leadership.

LEAKING VERSUS CHARGING

WHERE ENERGY GOES BEFORE PERFORMANCE

Most people think they're burned out because of workload, intensity, or physical exhaustion. In reality, many performers and leaders are not tired from what they've done—they are tired from what they've been leaking.

You're not always energy-depleted. Sometimes you're energy-drained before you even begin. A warrior doesn't just ask themselves, *Do I have enough energy?* They ask, *Where am I losing energy before it even converts into performance?*

THE DIFFERENCE: ENERGY DRAINS VERSUS ENERGY DEMANDS

ENERGY DEMANDS (NECESSARY OUTPUT)	ENERGY LEAKS (UNNECESSARY DEPLETION)
Physical Performance	Worry about your outcomes
Focused Thinking	Scattered thought loops
Intentional Emotional Expression	Emotional overreactions
Team Support (with boundaries)	Carrying everyone's feelings
Work or Sport Execution	Overanticipation or forecast anxiety
Tactical Breathing	Unconscious shallow chest breathing
Composed Body Readiness	Constant tension in shoulders or jaw
Active Problem-Solving	Replaying regrets

WHAT LEAKS ENERGY THE FASTEST?

Here are some of the biggest hidden drains you may not realize are costing you performance capacity:

LEAK CATEGORY	EXAMPLE	IMPACT
Emotional Rumination	"What if I fail?" loops	Burns glucose and spikes cortisol
Decision Fatigue	Constant micro-decisions with no system	Cognitive drain
Overthinking	Replaying mistakes	Mental overheating
Muscle Tension	Locked jaw Stiff posture	Burns oxygen and increases fatigue
Anticipation Without Action	Thinking about doing more than taking action	Wasted readiness
Carrying Others' Stress	Absorbing rather than anchoring	Nervous system overload
Unfiltered Environment	Negative chatter Energy vampires	Emotional erosion
Poor Breathing	Moving from overbreathing to CO_2 blow-off to panic	Fast fatigue

Charging is not just rest—it's regeneration. Many athletes and leaders think rest alone restores energy. But if the body is still breathing inefficiently, carrying silent anxiety, and staying in fight-or-flight internally, rest is just paused stress.

True charging activates parasympathetic restoration and restores energy through:

- Deep diaphragmatic breathing
- Rhythmic movement to release tension
- Emotional decompression after intensity
- Micro-recovery cycles during long efforts
- Environmental resets (space away from noise)
- Purposeful reconnection to emotional energy regeneration

Warriors focus on closing leaks first, then on generating efficient energy output.

HOW THIS SUPPORTS YOUR PERFORMANCE OS

PERFORMANCE OS ELEMENT	SHIFT
Energy	You reclaim wasted capacity and redirect it into execution.
Emotions	Emotional spirals no longer drain your energy before performance.
Environment	You intentionally remove people and spaces that leak stamina.
Warrior Identity	You see energy as a weapon to be preserved, not expended blindly.

FIELD NOTE EXAMPLE

A client once told me, "I'm exhausted every time I step onto the court." But after tracking their leak cycles, I discovered they were losing energy long before the warm-up: spiraling on match outcomes, checking social judgment, tensing shoulders on arrival, and breathing shallowly. Once those leaks were closed, they were no longer drained before they even began.

CLOSING SHIFT

Before asking how to go harder, ask yourself: *Where am I getting drained without even performing yet?*

YOU DON'T JUST LIVE IN ENVIRONMENTS: THEY LIVE IN YOU

SPACE SHAPES YOU

Most people assume they carry their mindset into every environment. In reality, environments often shape your mindset before you even begin. You don't just walk into a room. The room walks into you—through sensory cues, emotional memory, social pressure, and subconscious associations.

Some environments shrink your posture and quiet your voice. Others wake up your conviction, sharpen your focus, and make your breathing deeper without you realizing it. If you don't learn to consciously influence or recondition environments, they will unconsciously condition you. Every environment you enter is either:

- Charging you—improving your belief, rhythm, breathing, and posture.
- Neutral—it doesn't interfere.
- Draining you—triggering doubt, tension, fatigue, comparison, or fear.

Your body reacts before your logic can explain why.

WHY ENVIRONMENTS AFFECT YOUR PERFORMANCE OS SO QUICKLY

ENVIRONMENTAL FACTOR	WHAT YOUR BODY REGISTERS UNCONSCIOUSLY
Lighting and Space	When they're open, your body registers possibility. When they're closed, your body registers threats.
Noise Patterns	A chaotic room leads to internal agitation.
Temperature and Smell	These triggers are linked to memory.
Faces and People	Status dynamics trigger nervous system responses.
Past Emotional Memories	Remembering previous defeats leads to tension.

Emotional memory lives in places:

- A locker room tied to previous failure
- A boardroom where you were once challenged
- A childhood home filled with conflict
- A court where you've struggled

These places contain stored emotional meaning. Your nervous system remembers, even if your conscious mind has moved on. That's why the first few seconds in a space determine your trajectory there. If you enter without awareness, you often adapt to the room instead of leading it. If you enter with intention, you teach your body to hold its ground. If you recondition the environment, it begins to serve you rather than challenge you.

Warriors don't assume environment neutrality—they claim or recalibrate it. They:

- Don't enter spaces casually.
- Assess rhythm, tension, and energy.
- Reset the emotional memory linked to a location.
- Arrive with posture and breath that signal "I am not here to fit in—I am here to define my state."

WHAT SHIFTS IN YOUR PERFORMANCE OS

PERFORMANCE OS ELEMENT	ENVIRONMENTAL AWARENESS IMPACT
Energy	You begin shaping context rather than being shaped by it.
Emotions	You avoid unnecessary depletion from places that silently drain you.
Environment	You stop being emotionally triggered without understanding why.
Warrior Identity	You walk into rooms as someone who understands energy fields, not just social spaces.

FIELD STORY EXAMPLE

At times, Aryna stepped onto certain courts already tense. Her body remembered the previous losses from those environments. Once she redefined the emotional meaning of those spaces through ritual and intentional entry, they stopped being reminders of failure and reverted to neutral battlegrounds.

CLOSING SHIFT

Warriors don't just survive their environments; they recondition them. Once you understand that environments live inside your nervous system, you gain the power to rebuild them from the inside out.

WHY CERTAIN ROOMS MAKE YOU SMALL (AND HOW TO RECLAIM THEM)

THE SHRINKING REFLEX

There are rooms you'll walk into where you'll immediately stand smaller, speak softer, second-guess your worth, or feel as if you're behind before anything even starts. It may be a boardroom, a locker room, a competitive arena, a childhood home, or even a digital environment where certain voices live.

This shrinking is not always conscious or logical. It's a neurological and emotional response to your environment. If you don't learn how to detect and recondition these spaces, they'll quietly dictate your posture, breathing, thoughts, and decisions—often before you take your first action.

WHY ENVIRONMENTS CAN MAKE YOU FEEL SMALL

TRIGGER	WHY IT AFFECTS YOU
Past failure in that space	Your body remembers being under threat there.
Power dynamics in the room	Your nervous system tracks social hierarchy automatically.
Eyes on you	Perceived judgment activates your survival networks.
Tight spatial restriction (small room)	Triggers a trapped or constrained response.
Unfamiliar setting	Your brain conserves energy and preps for uncertainty.
History of conflict in that space	Your body braces subconsciously for confrontation.

Even before you speak, your breathing may rise, your rib cage may tighten, your chin may drop—all signs that your nervous system is preparing for threat rather than performance.

There are two common reactions:

- You shrink to stay unnoticed.
- You overcompensate with forced confidence or aggression.

Both responses are reactions to environmental pressure. The warrior's mindset shift: You can't always adjust the environment, but you can recalibrate how you occupy it.

- You don't demand dominance.
- You don't fake confidence.
- You establish presence quietly but firmly through posture, breath, groundedness, and an intentional entry ritual.

Once you physically reestablish agency, your nervous system begins to perceive the space as belonging to you, not threatening you.

HOW TO RECLAIM A SPACE (4-STEP WARRIOR RECONDITIONING)

STEP	WHAT TO DO	WHY IT WORKS
1. Pause at the entry.	Stop before entering a space to prevent unconscious adaptation.	Creates an intentional threshold moment.
2. Ground and breathe.	Take one low inhale and release a controlled exhale (4 counts in, 6 out).	Signals safety and self-possession.
3. Expand posture slightly.	Broaden your chest, align your spine, and relax your jaw.	Posture affects your hormones and your emotional readiness.
4. Choose an identity phrase.	"I don't adapt to the room—I bring my state here." "I belong here because I came prepared."	Sets internal authority.

This will anchor your body in the space.

WHAT SHIFTS IN YOUR PERFORMANCE OS

PERFORMANCE OS ELEMENT	SHIFT
Energy	You stop bleeding energy into subconscious fear.
Emotions	Your anxiety becomes manageable as your safety perception increases.
Environment	The space goes from dominant to neutral or even supportive.
Warrior Identity	You move from visitor to presence holder.

The room only makes you small when you let it define your place in it. You have the power to let your state reshape the place.

Appendix III—The Notes: Personal Reflections and Letters from the Field

WHEN PANIC MAKES YOU DOUBT YOUR READINESS

It starts in the chest.

A flicker, then a surge. You feel it in your fingers, in the shallow edge of your breath, in the heat that climbs your neck. Suddenly, the body you've trained for years doesn't feel like home anymore. It's foreign. Electric. Unpredictable. Every thought sounds louder than your pulse, and the noise convinces you something's wrong.

But nothing's broken. What you're feeling is the body doing its job *too* well. It's preparing you to survive, even though you're trying to perform. Panic is just energy without direction.

Panic doesn't mean you're unprepared. It means you're ready, but unregulated. You've built the strength. You've put in the hours. The system just needs a signal that it's safe to proceed.

So, start with your breath. Inhale through the nose, long and low, until you feel your ribs expand. Exhale slowly enough for the noise to thin. You aren't training to erase panic, nor is panic the enemy. You're simply acknowledging it and letting it move through you. Panic trapped in the chest becomes fear. Panic, given a pathway, becomes focus.

As the air steadies, the world will sharpen again, revealing the details you missed when the noise took over: the weight of your feet, the shape of the space you're in, the sound of your breath filling the silence. These are your coordinates back to your center. You can't think your way to calm. You have to feel your way there.

And when the chaos softens—but doesn't disappear—you'll understand what most people never learn: Readiness isn't the absence of panic but the ability to navigate within it. The body will still hum. The pulse will still race. But you will be in control.

WHEN MISTAKES REPLAY LOUDER THAN YOUR BREATH

It happens fast. You make a mistake, and suddenly it's the only thing in your head. You replay it like a broken loop, convinced that if you run it again, you'll find the frame where everything went wrong. But that's not how memory works. The mind doesn't rewind to learn; it rewinds to punish.

I've seen that look before—eyes fixed in the distance, body still moving through the motions while the brain keeps shouting, *How could I?* The truth is that the mistake isn't the problem. The fixation is the problem. Every second spent replaying what already happened is a second spent practicing hesitation. And hesitation will become a habit faster than you expect.

When you stay in that loop long enough, you start to believe the error defines you. You forget it was just one frame in a much larger film. The body moves how it's been trained; the mind follows whatever it's fed.

Feed it guilt, and it slows.

Feed it awareness, and it learns.

The choice sounds simple, but under pressure, simplicity feels like a luxury.

The next time that loop starts, interrupt it. Don't analyze—just breathe. Feel your feet. Let the body pull you back into the present. Because the body is always in the now—it doesn't care what happened 10 seconds ago. If you can return there, even for a breath, you'll notice how the noise starts to fade.

So, when the noise starts to rise again, when your mind starts pulling old tapes from the shelf, remember this: The replay isn't the lesson, the reset is. Breathe once. Feel your feet. Lift your eyes up. Move forward.

WHEN PRESSURE CONVINCES YOU EMOTIONS EQUAL WEAKNESS

Pressure will rewrite the rules. It will tell you that composure means silence, that strength means stillness, that emotion is a crack instead of a current. It will make you believe that the only way to stay in control is to lock everything down.

But emotion is how your body communicates the truth. It's easy to think that suppressing your emotions will erase them, but instead, you'll just drive them deeper into the system until they leak out sideways as fatigue, distraction, or doubt.

When pressure rises, you'll be tempted to clamp down, to go flat and convince yourself you're fine. But if you can stay open—even slightly—you'll notice something different. Beneath the noise and adrenaline, there are signals.

The nerves before a performance are your system saying, *This matters.*

The lump in your throat after a loss is your body confirming that you cared.

I've yet to meet an athlete, leader, fighter, or parent who felt nothing under pressure. The best performers are the ones who've learned to stay open anyway.

WHEN EXHAUSTION FEELS LIKE FAILURE

There's a type of tired that even sleep won't touch. It settles in behind your eyes and stays there, even after the body stops moving. It's a fatigue that comes when you've done everything right—hit the reps, followed the plan, carried the weight—and still feel empty. That's the exhaustion no one prepares you for. It whispers in your ear and makes you think, *Maybe I've lost it.*

But exhaustion isn't proof of weakness. It's the body's last honest message—its way of saying, *You've been running too far from yourself.* It shows up when the system's been in survival mode too long. When output has outpaced recovery. When you've been performing at full volume with no pause to let the echo fade.

The body, like the mind, has seasons. Ignore them long enough, and even your best effort turns brittle. So, when exhaustion hits, don't treat it like failure. Treat it like feedback. It's not asking you to quit; it's asking you to listen. You've been holding your breath too long, running on adrenaline instead of rhythm. The reset doesn't come from another burst of effort—it comes from release.

Start with stillness. Ten minutes in a dark room. A walk without music. A breath that doesn't have to count toward anything. Let the noise drain until the silence no longer feels heavy but comfortable. That's the moment recovery starts.

WHEN FOCUS FRACTURES UNDER NOISE

It doesn't take much to lose the thread.

A single distraction, a glance, a sound you didn't expect, and suddenly the mind scatters like a flock of birds startled from a wire. You might try to chase it, pulling the pieces back together, but the harder you reach, the faster it slips.

Noise always finds its way in. Sometimes it's external—the pull of the crowd, the hum of expectation. Sometimes it's internal—the echo of unfinished thoughts, the quiet doubt you thought you'd outgrown. Either way, it lives in the same place: between your awareness and your breath. You can't fight it with force. You have to soften until the noise runs out of room to land.

There's a difference between concentration and control. Control burns energy just trying to hold itself together. But concentration—real focus—is open. It's a presence, not a prison. Concentration isn't keeping every distracting thought out. Instead, it's simply letting the thoughts flow in and out. Though it may seem counterintuitive, the more you try to keep out distractions, the more your mind hangs onto them.

When focus fractures, don't rush to rebuild it. Pause. Feel the edges of your awareness. Let your attention spread out instead of closing in. The mind will try to contract around the mistake or the sound or the doubt, but the more space you give it, the less grip it has. Let the distraction flow out, and your focus will return in a quiet tide. The depth will deepen. The noise will dull. The distractions will fade.

That's focus. Not the narrow beam of a spotlight, but the wide calm of awareness that sees everything and chooses where to rest.

You won't hold it forever. No one does. But the point was never permanence—it was remembering how to return. To lose yourself a hundred times, and a hundred times find your way back, each return a little quicker, and a little gentler, than the one before.

TO THE ONE LEARNING TO TRUST STILLNESS

You've spent so long sprinting toward the next thing that you've started to mistake movement for progress. There's always been another hill, another opponent, another scoreboard flashing somewhere in your mind. You've lived off motion the way some people live off caffeine—running on the quiet fear that if you ever stop, you might not start again.

But every fighter who stays in the game long enough eventually learns that stillness is a strategy. The body needs recovery the way metal needs cooling. And if you can't stop, you can't sharpen.

At first, stillness feels like punishment. You sit there, every muscle coiled, mind clawing for something to fix. The silence gets loud. You start hearing things you've been too busy to notice—the rough scrape of your breath in your throat, the low hum of the lights, the faint rhythm of your pulse in your wrists. It's uncomfortable because it's honest. Stillness doesn't flatter you; it confronts you. It shows you the difference between strength and speed, between noise and signal.

Pressure will always try to convince you that movement is safety. It tells you to act, to push, to do something. But pressure is like water—it responds to shape, not shouting. The more you thrash, the more it takes from you. The more you settle, the more you can start to feel its current. Control is about learning to move without wasting motion.

There's a quiet power that comes when you stop performing urgency. When you can stand in the middle of chaos without flinching, when you can feel your heartbeat without trying to slow it down. When you stop chasing the noise, you start hearing the signal again—the small, steady rhythm underneath it all. That's your center. That's where the real strength lives.

So, sit still, even when it feels unnatural. Let the silence rearrange things. Let the noise fall away until what's left is breath, heartbeat, pulse. And when you move again, don't move just to move but instead with intention.

WHEN CONFIDENCE FALTERS MID-CLIMB

There's a moment, somewhere past the halfway point, when belief starts to slip.

You look down and realize how far you've come, then up and see how far there still is to go, and the air between those two distances feels thinner than you remembered. The body hesitates. The mind starts doing the math. Every movement that used to feel fluid now feels fragile, like the smallest mistake could send you backward.

Doubt is sneaky. It arrives disguised as logic. It asks questions that sound reasonable: *Are you sure? What if you're wrong? Who do you think you are?* And before you realize it, you've turned from moving to analyzing. But you can't think your way out of doubt. You can only move your way through it.

Every system has a point where it needs recalibration. The body isn't a machine, but it speaks in the same language—fatigue, hesitation, misfires. None of these are failures; they're signals.

When confidence wavers, pause—but not to justify your fear. Pause to breathe, to feel the weight of your own hands, the steadiness still available underneath the noise. You don't have to find full certainty to take the next step; you just have to find enough. Confidence is the quiet decision to keep climbing. Because the climb was never about height. It was about the return—about finding your footing again after the slip, finding your breath again after the gasp, and finding your center again after the noise.

You were built to keep going.

TO THE ONE WHO'S LEARNING TO MOVE AGAIN

The hardest part about falling isn't getting back up; it's taking the next step forward. Getting up is simply returning yourself to baseline. But when you take that step forward, you're choosing to keep moving. To keep trying. And sometimes, that step can feel impossible.

Your system remembers pain more clearly than victory, and it's trying to protect you. But inaction can calcify. The same instinct that shields you can also keep you from ever moving forward. If you wait for safety, if you wait for certainty, you will never take that first step. The only way to start moving again is to move from that place of uncertainty—to move, even when you're terrified that you are just going to fall again.

At first, the movements will be clumsy, heavy. You'll reach for a rhythm and find only fragments of one. You will be tempted to push harder—to tighten your grip and prove you're in control. Resist. Control born from fear only locks the gears of progress. Loosen up a little. Breathe. Let that breath create some space around you. And then keep moving.

The early steps may feel graceless, but they're the most important steps you'll ever take. Each one repairs the signal between mind and body. Your rhythm will trickle back—a pulse here, a clean landing there—until one day, movement feels less like effort and more like remembering.

You won't ever move the same way you did in the past. Your architecture has fundamentally changed. The rebuilt version of you wastes fewer emotions and carries a clearer sense of direction.

Where there was once drive, there is now discipline. Every step is more precise, intentional.

So, take the step.

It's not a leap. It's not a performance. It's just one measured stride toward the next moment.

Move—not to prove you're unbreakable, but because breaking taught you how to bend.

Acknowledgments

This book exists because two journeys finally came together.

One was lived over decades.

The other only became possible because of the people who helped translate that life into words.

PART I: THE LIFE THAT SHAPED THE WORK

Before there was a book, there was a life that had to be survived, shaped, and rebuilt.

My father was a hard man. A veteran. Firm in his values and uncompromising in his standards. He set the bar early, and even after he passed, that bar never moved. His voice stayed with me.

My mother did everything she could in an impossible situation. After my father passed, she carried far more than anyone should have to, and she did it quietly, relentlessly, and with a strength I only fully understand now.

My brother has always been resilient and loyal. Still standing. Still solid.

My sister—rest in peace. A beautiful soul whose life didn't end with her. Through organ donation, she saved others. Years later, the recipient of her heart reached out because she was still living on. That truth never leaves me.

Then there were the people who changed the trajectory of my life completely.

The Patawarans gave me more than I could ever repay. They didn't just help—they saved my life. They gave me structure, safety, discipline, and a living example of what a strong family looks like when you [illegible] most. That was the final shift that helped me see there was more to life, and so much worth living for.

Tony, the father—hardworking, steady, always doing everything he could for his family. He invited me in without hesitation and taught me more than he probably realized.

Margaret, the mother—kind, caring, and one of the strongest people I've ever known. She's endured more than most and never lost her heart.

Jen, the eldest—driven and disciplined in school and sport. She supported me through my early years of study, volunteered as a very willing guinea pig, and kept showing up. She's now a physiotherapist and still absolutely crushing it.

Amanda—independent, loving, strong, and no BS. We've always been close, but in recent years she's been relentless in the best way—pushing me to believe in myself, to value what I do, and to finally see what others see in me. I don't think this book happens without her encouragement.

Amy, the youngest—the free spirit. Always reminding me to slow down, enjoy life, and remember that it's all shorter than we think. I still see her as that energetic young girl who trusted me completely and reminded me not to miss what matters.

Jan gave me community, purpose, and direction when I needed it most. He helped build a stronger, more curious mind and introduced me to the people who would become family—the Patawarans, Tom, and Jeremy.

Tom became a brother and a mentor.

Jeremy became a brother through challenge, pressure, and countless hours on the mats beating the hell out of each other and becoming better because of it.

Big Al was a gentle giant. A leader from the start. Kind, steady, and supportive in a way that made strength feel safe.

Charlene challenged me on so many levels and helped me begin my path to healing and true growth. She allowed me to open up and be free. I'm glad I was able to say goodbye before she passed—I still hear her voice guiding me to this day.

There are many others, but these are the ones from back in the day—the people who shaped me when it mattered most.

Renee, my former wife, and the mother of my three youngest children—Aidan, Kai, and Jada. While we're no longer together, she supported the work, the travel, the long hours, and helped raise our kids into the people they're becoming. That deserves respect and acknowledgment.

Every person named here cared about me for who I am—not just what I do. That distinction changed everything.

And of course to Aryna and Anton. We've been through lots together and this thing we've built is something special. I'm proud to know you and call you family.

PART II: THE PEOPLE WHO MADE THE BOOK POSSIBLE

A life lived doesn't automatically become a book. It takes others to help shape it, challenge it, and carry it into the world.

James Laughlin started this entire thing. I never would have written a book if he hadn't decided to help get me out there. He opened the door.

Scott Miller connected the dots. He saw the value, made the introductions, and helped turn possibility into momentum.

Platte Clark did an enormous amount of work bringing structure, flow, and clarity to what was often raw and unfiltered. He helped organize the madness without stripping away the truth. The Performance OS is the clearest example—a solid, usable framework that everything could wrap around.

Kennidy Clark strengthened the writing, checked and found sources, and brought a sharp editorial eye and perspective throughout the process. Her care, honesty, and attention made this book materially better.

Matt Holt took a chance on me. That mattered. Belief turned into action, and action turned into a finished book.

Without this group, I'd still be doing what I love—coaching, pushing, helping people perform—but I wouldn't be building, sharing, or growing this work beyond the room I was standing in.

FINALLY, TO MY FAMILY

Kellee, Aidan, Kai, and Jada.

You are the reason the work has limits. The reason success is never the point by itself. You remind me daily of what matters most, whether you mean to or not.

Everything I build, I build with you in mind. Not just results—but a life that's worth living inside of.

This book carries that intention forward.

Notes

1. "Circadian Rhythms," National Institute of General Medical Sciences, accessed February 9, 2026, https://www.nigms.nih.gov/education/fact-sheets/Pages/circadian-rhythms.
2. M. P. Gerkema, "Ultradian Rhythms," *Biological Rhythms* (2002): 207–15, https://doi.org/10.1007/978-3-662-06085-8_17.
3. Pamela Dalton, Christopher Maute, Cristina Jaén, and Tamika Wilson, "Chemosignals of Stress Influence Social Judgments," *PLOS One* 8, no. 10 (2013): e77144, https://doi.org/10.1371/journal.pone.0077144; J. Zhou and W. Chen, "Human Chemosensory Communication of Fear and Happiness," *Emotion* 9, no. 2 (2009): 135–143, https://doi.org/10.1037/a0017846.
4. C. Styliadis, A. A. Ioannides, P. D. Bamidis, and C. Papadelis, "Mapping the Spatiotemporal Evolution of Emotional Processing," *Frontiers in Human Neuroscience*, 12 (2018): 1–17, https://doi.org/10.3389/fnhum.2018.00322; Mark Travers, "A Psychologist Shares the '90-Second Rule' to Survive Emotional Waves," *Forbes*, March 10, 2025, https://www.forbes.com/sites/traversmark/2025/03/10/a-psychologist-shares-the-90-second-rule-to-survive-emotional-waves/.
5. Kurt Lewin and Fritz Heider, *Principles of Topological Psychology* (McGraw-Hill, 1936).
6. María Kathia Cárdenas, Catherine P. Benzinger, Timesh D. Pillay, and J. Jaime Miranda, "The Effect of Changes in Visibility and Price on Fruit Purchasing

at a University Cafeteria in Lima, Peru," *Public Health Nutrition* 18, no. 15 (December 1, 2014): 2742–49, https://doi.org/10.1017/s1368980014002730.

7. Tyler W. Watts, Greg J. Duncan, and Haonan Quan, "Revisiting the Marshmallow Test: A Conceptual Replication Investigating Links Between Early Delay of Gratification and Later Outcomes," *Psychological Science* 29, no. 7 (2018): 1159–77, https://doi.org/10.1177/0956797618761661.
8. Julianne Holt-Lunstad, Timothy B. Smith, and J. Bradley Layton, "Social Relationships and Mortality Risk: A Meta-analytic Review," *PLOS Medicine* 7, no. 7 (July 27, 2010), https://doi.org/10.1371/journal.pmed.1000316.
9. Jasper H. B. de Groot and Monique A. M. Smeets, "Human Fear Chemosignaling: Evidence from a Meta-Analysis," *Chemical Senses* 42, no. 8 (October 2017): 663–73, https://doi.org/10.1093/chemse/bjx049; Pamela Dalton et al., "Chemosignals of Stress Influence Social Judgments," *PLOS One* 8, no. 10 (2013): e77144, https://doi.org/10.1371/journal.pone.0077144; Alexander W. J. Freemantle, Lorenzo D. Stafford, Christopher R. D. Wagstaff, and Lucy Akehurst, "The Relationship Between Olfactory Function and Emotional Contagion," *Chemosensory Perception* 15 (2022): 49–59, https://doi.org/10.1007/s12078-021-09293-4.
10. Naoki Konishi, Motohiro Kimura, Ken Kihara, et al., "Psychological Richness as a Distinct Dimension of Well-Being: Links to Mental, Social, and Physical Health," *PLOS One* 20, no. 6 (June 18, 2025), https://doi.org/10.1371/journal.pone.0326528.
11. Jonne O. Hietanen, Mikko J. Peltola, and Jari K. Hietanen, "Psychophysiological Responses to Eye Contact in a Live Interaction and in Video Call," *Psychophysiology* 57, no. 6 (April 22, 2020), https://doi.org/10.1111/psyp.13587.
12. Ajay B. Satpute and Kristen A. Lindquist, "At the Neural Intersection Between Language and Emotion," *Affective Science* 2, no. 2 (March 20, 2021): 207–20, https://doi.org/10.1007/s42761-021-00032-2.
13. Wen Li and Andreas Keil, "Sensing Fear: Fast and Precise Threat Evaluation in Human Sensory Cortex," *Trends in Cognitive Sciences* 27, no. 4 (April 2023): 341–52, https://doi.org/10.1016/j.tics.2023.01.001; W. Clinton McSherry and Jeffrey E. Holm, "Sense of Coherence: Its Effects on Psychological and Physiological Processes Prior to, During, and After a Stressful Situation," *Journal of Clinical Psychology* 50, no. 4 (July 1994): 476–87, https://doi.org/10.1002/1097-4679(199407)50:4<476::AID-JCLP2270500402>3.0.CO;2-9; Bruce H. Lipton, *The Biology of Belief: Unleashing the Power of Consciousness, Matter, & Miracles*, 10th Anniversary ed. (Hay House, 2015).
14. Melis Yilmaz Balban et al., "Brief Structured Respiration Practices Enhance Mood and Reduce Physiological Arousal," *Cell Reports Medicine* 4, no. 1 (January 2023): 100895, https://doi.org/10.1016/j.xcrm.2022.100895.

About the Author

Photo by Unbox Sports/Felipe Figueiredo

Jason Stacy is a world-class high-performance coach and international speaker who helps elite athletes, coaches, and high-stakes leaders integrate physical mastery, mental clarity, and emotional regulation to achieve and sustain success at the highest level. With over three decades of experience, he has coached Olympic, world, and national champions in tennis, combat sports, professional dance, swimming, gymnastics, and more—including Aryna Sabalenka, World No. 1 and multiple Grand Slam champion. Jason's work has been featured in Netflix's *Break Point*, ESPN, *Good Morning America*, and on stages around the globe.

MORE WAYS TO ENGAGE JASON

Jason is available for a variety of performance-related coaching and consultations.

CONTACT JASON'S TEAM AT: **thepressurecode.com**

1 KEYNOTES & SPECIAL EVENTS

Jason Stacy delivers high-impact keynotes that teach audiences how to operate with clarity, control, and energy in high pressure environments. His message applies to world-class athletes, business leaders, and any team facing intense demands.

2 PERFORMANCE COACHING

Jason Stacy is the mental and physical performance coach behind elite performers, from Grand Slam champions to CEOs who operate at the edge of their capacity. His work turns pressure from something people fear into something they can use with precision.

3 TAKE THE FIGHTER TO WARRIOR AUDIT

A state-based performance diagnostic.

SCAN THIS CODE TO TAKE THE WARRIOR AUDIT FOR FREE

NOT WHO YOU ARE.
HOW YOU OPERATE UNDER PRESSURE.

Fourteen questions. Two dimensions. One honest snapshot of your operating system when the stakes are real.